MW01121948

The Many Faces Of Evil

Reflections On The Sinful,
The Tragic, The Demonic,
And The Ambiguous

Kenneth Cauthen

CSS Publishing Company, Inc., Lima, Ohio

THE MANY FACES OF EVIL

Library of Congress Cataloging-in-Publication Data

Cauthen, Kenneth, 1930-
    The many faces of evil : reflections on the sinful, the tragic, the demonic, and the
ambiguous / Kenneth Cauthen.
        p.   cm.
    Includes bibliographical references and index.
    ISBN 0-7880-1004-2
    1. Good and evil. I. Title.
BJ1401.C32   1997
230—dc20   96-38674
                                                                            CIP

ISBN: 0-7880-1004-2   PRINTED IN U.S.A.

To

Nancy Beulah Harris Cauthen

December 26, 1909-

*How fortunate I
am to have this
wonderful woman
for my mother.*

Table of Contents

Preface

Every author's ambition is to write a book that appeals to everybody. I am not an exception. Most of my writing has been for theological students and specialists in religion and philosophy. Without neglecting them, I have on this occasion made a deliberate attempt to appeal to a wider audience. My aim is to understand the many faces of evil as completely and as deeply as possible. This requires the construction of enough theory to serve that purpose. However, I have written as simply and as intelligibly as I can. Moreover, I have constantly made references to everyday life to illustrate my points and to pose the questions I seek to answer. I hope this will invite the attention of laypeople with an interest in understanding and coping with evil but disinterested in extended technical discussions of the issue. Total success in such an effort requires gifts I have only in part. I cannot escape that aspect of my training and innate inclination that aspires to systematic analysis of issues. I hope, however, I have made my definitions and classifications in language that is sufficiently down to earth and comprehensible to be of interest to non-specialists and yet precise enough to indicate to scholars where I stand on the theological and philosophical spectrum.

I have made copious and constant mention of events taken from newspapers and from my own experience in order to keep close to actual life in the home, the church, the hospital, the marketplace, and the world of politics. Nearly every chapter begins with a story with which everyone can identify. At times my language has the simplicity of conversation and at other points takes on the more formal tone of the theological essay. My aim is to be as lucid as possible and yet not to avoid the difficulties and complexities with which serious thought must engage. With this introduction to style, let me proceed to content.

Evil is not the only challenge human beings face in this life, but nothing is more pervasive or perplexing. When we combine all the forms of pain, anguish, want, disease, accident, catastrophe, violent conflict, tragic and premature death, injustice, emotional distress, spiritual despair, and all the other ills that devastate and destroy body, mind, and soul, everyone is touched or tormented in some fashion. Evil is, of course, not one big problem but a multitude of particular impediments to fullness of life.

Evil is in part the measure of our moral delinquency. Many of our afflictions are the consequence of our failures to support each other in the effort to achieve the good life in all its dimensions and varieties. Our human vocation is to promote the highest possible fulfillment of the potential for pleasure, happiness, and joy of which every person is capable. Because of our misdeeds and our neglect we fall far short of achieving the best that could be for all people. By our destructive and often violent assaults on each other, as well as by our indifference and carelessness, we are responsible for much of the misery and sorrow that cover the earth with blood and tears. Individuals harm and destroy each other in personal relationships. Societies organize themselves for the advantage of some and the detriment of others. Races, classes, cultures, and nations engage in destructive conflicts with each other. Iniquities arising in one generation create a demonic power that lives on in the lives of individuals and social institutions until a countervailing force of good does its liberating work.

Not all suffering results from human dereliction, of course. Much grief and tribulation arise out of nature, the fact that we are vulnerable creatures of flesh and blood — finite beings. (1) We are subject to annihilation by external forces that devastate our

8

bodies and spirits from without. Bacteria, viruses, fire, water, wind, earthquakes, stones, and other damaging objects assault the body from without. (2) We are also susceptible to breakdowns of the organic systems within us. Genetic defects and the malfunctioning of molecules, cells, and organs inside our bodies lead to pain, physical diseases, mental disorders, and death. Hence, even if we all did our utmost to achieve the best that could be for everybody, much suffering would still occur. It is unavoidable as a consequence of the vulnerability that accompanies the fact that we are finite bodies immersed in a natural world whose laws and processes operate inexorably to produce hurt, sickness, ruin, and extinction.

Other impediments to the totally good life arise out of the very fact of imperfection and limitation associated with the finite world. Some are related to the nature of time and space. This may be the occasion of at least frustration if not actual suffering that we need to worry much about. For example, we cannot be at two different places at the same time when we might desperately want to. It is impossible for all baseball fans to be physically in attendance at the World Series with seats close enough to the playing field to make it worthwhile. Not everyone who might want to can live close enough to an airport to be convenient and far enough way to avoid the noise and crowds.

More serious is the fact that all the just aims of people in a complex society cannot always be coordinated without loss. Some compromise is necessary. Since some values conflict with others, even the most just policies possible will in some instances help some while hurting others. A constant threat to perfect outcomes is this intertwining of good and evil so that we cannot separate them out to preserve the good and eliminate the evil. Hence, life in many respects is morally ambiguous. Maximizing freedom in a society is likely to produce great inequalities. Increasing equality for all will require putting limits on the freedom of some. Examples of the moral ambiguity related to tension between competing values are too numerous to list or even classify. The fact that human beings can experience a broader and deeper range of intense pleasures and joys than elephants means that they are also capable of greater suffering and frustration. Such is our lot in this life that we cannot have the pleasant and the satisfying without the risk and the fact of the painful and the displeasing.

Still other evils are tragic because they are unavoidable under the circumstances for those involved and in the nature of the case irredeemable. A family cannot devote the necessary attention and funds to a chronically ill child without the risk of depriving their other offspring emotionally and financially. Given access to medical treatments available today, both my grandfathers could have had many more years of useful life. Women born in previous generations were denied opportunities open to their daughters and granddaughters by the mere accident of timing. Roman Catholic women called to priestly ministry are in this generation bound to suffer no matter what choices they make. Children born into poverty through no fault of their own are denied pleasures and hopes readily available to their more affluent contemporaries.

Then there are the many ironies, contradictions, and ambiguities associated with the way history actually occurred. African-Americans brought here in chains suffered deprivations that their descendants, while still facing enormous barriers of prejudice and hostility, will never undergo. Ironically, since they were born in this country because their slave ancestors were brought here forcibly, they may have opportunities denied their contemporary African cousins whose forebears remained free of enslavement by white people of European descent. Voluntary immigration to America over the last four centuries provided millions of Europeans escape from tyranny, poverty, and hopelessness, but in the process of seeking a better life for themselves, they destroyed Native American peoples and cultures. So it goes with good and evil alternately causing and eliminating and entangling themselves with each other in ways that endlessly surprise, baffle, and torment us.

In short, we want and seek the good, but factors rooted in human failure (freedom) and in the nature of things (finitude) produce evils galore as inevitable accompaniments of our human quest for enjoyment, health, security, and happiness. This little book will explore many of the forms and sources of suffering that spring from one or the other or some combination of freedom and finitude. My aim is to investigate evil in its major dimensions, not only to understand that it is a pervasive and unavoidable feature of life but also to examine suffering in light of religious faith. It is the product of many years of reflection, but I am acutely aware of its limits in the face of the challenge posed by the issues tackled.

The thinking that goes into each chapter is done within a liberal Christian framework. Central to the issues I discuss is the relation of our suffering to the activity and purpose of God. My own deliberations will be found to be inadequate to some by offering less than a full, robust Christian faith has traditionally provided. I try to make clear why I find it necessary to reinterpret the way God operates within the world to achieve the divine aims. It is made available to others who have not found the typical approaches to theodicy satisfactory in the light of their own experiences and reflections. To traditionalists, I can only say that my project is an honest effort to find a better way, not an exercise in criticism and rejection for its own sake.

In the background of my thinking is a version of process-relational thought. Many followers of that path, more faithful in their orthodoxy than I, will not find nearly enough exegesis of Alfred North Whitehead with his distinctive vocabulary to satisfy their own proclivities. I am a shameless eclectic who uses whatever insights I can find from whatever source to make sense of things. Nevertheless, the general theory of the world I find in Whitehead informs me at a deep level, although increasingly I do not worry about the details of the magnificent edifice he constructed in his many works. Anyone who is interested may peruse some of my other books where my identification with process theology is more explicit and detailed.

I am indebted to more people, books, student seminars, and conversations than I could ever list here. In the end, however, the point of view that fills these pages is my own, and I take full responsibility for it. My hope is that it may be of value to other searchers who seek both insight and inspiration in contending with our greatest challenge.

Kenneth Cauthen
Rochester, New York
July 31, 1996

Chapter One

The Approach:
Does Thinking About Evil Help?

*No statement, theological or otherwise, should be made
that would not be credible in the presence of burning
children.*

Irving Greenberg[1]

If it be true that no theological statement should be made that
would not be believable in the presence of burning children, then
this provision certainly holds for assertions about evil. I hope that
what I say here lives up to that standard.

Evil has many faces. The common element in all evil is
suffering, but we need four other major categories to deal with its
manifold dimensions: the sinful, the tragic, the demonic, and the
ambiguous. Briefly put, the sinful refers to a wrongful use of
freedom that (1) distorts relationships with God and others and (2)
has harmful consequences. Its social expression is injustice. The
tragic characterizes suffering to the extent that it is unavoidable
and/or irredeemable. The demonic is the destructive power of the
past embodied presently in personality formation and social
structures. The ambiguous indicates the mixture of good and evil
in events and choices.

To these four could be added another. The fifth is ignorance.
Sometimes anguish and harm result not from carelessness or bad
intention but from sincere erroneous belief or simple lack of

13

knowledge or skill. I will not develop this point, since it would appear to be obvious and thus not in need of elaboration. I will refer to ignorance only in passing.

Moreover, a full accounting of life would require the opposites of the categories I have used to identify the many faces of evil. Not only are wrongdoing and injustice present in life, so are love and fairness. Not only is the demonic a troubler from the past, the angelic is blessing from the past, those humanly-created good influences woven into the structures of individual and social life that work themselves through the generations to enlighten and uplift. Not only is there tragedy, there is also the fortunate, grace, those fortuitous, propitious, and serendipitous occurrences that happen to us that enhance life beyond what we deserve. Not only must we wrestle with those ambiguous trade-offs in life, sometimes we enjoy unequivocal benefaction or suffer from an absolute curse. Not only do we harm each other out of ignorance, we also are able to do good because of our knowledge. This other side of the coin of life will not be detailed here, but these opposite factors are as real and as important as what I have attempted to delineate.

Several questions are central to the discussion. What do we mean by evil? Why is evil a part of our world? How is evil related to suffering? How does human freedom function to create and to conquer evil? What is God's responsibility in causing and overcoming evil? How should we understand divine power and goodness in relationship to suffering? These topics will be explored.

"Through many dangers, toils, and snares, we have already come," says that wonderful hymn we like to sing. Evil and suffering are never far from us. If we are not struggling with some affliction ourselves right now, it is likely that a member of the family or someone we know is. We need practical ways to cope with our anguish, to endure, and to overcome. For many that is enough. Others, like myself, long for understanding as well. The present effort is directed to those who need insight as well as comfort. I propose to take the risk of dealing theoretically with the question, fully aware that any such attempt may at best seem remote from life and beside the point. At worst the effort could become tedious and boring.

How can the analysis of evil and the outlining of possible views be of help to people who are suffering? Is thinking about it of any value? It is certainly true that thought can get detached from life and become irrelevant, but it need not be that way. Let me suggest a general principle that may be helpful. Alfred North Whitehead says, "The elucidation of immediate experience is the sole justification for any thought."[2] The purpose of thinking is to interpret experience. The basic reason for reflection is to seek answers for questions arising out of everyday existence. The aim of thought is to make sense out of life. Hence, the starting point must be real life experiences. And the ending point must come back to experience. The focus, first and last, of thought that is worth undertaking is ordinary life as it is lived day by day in the kitchen and in the marketplace and on the street.

To quote Whitehead again, *the function of Reason is to promote the art of life*.[3] In that same book, he writes that all living things are driven "by a three-fold urge: (i) to live, (ii) to live well, (iii) to live better. In fact, the art of life is *first* to be alive, *secondly* to be alive in a satisfactory way, and *thirdly* to acquire an increase in satisfaction."[4] The reason for thinking is to make life better, to provide guidance in daily living. Thinking is a practical enterprise. Theology seems irrelevant to a lot of people because the connection with experience is lost. Losing touch with the questions real people are asking and failing to make contact with the implications of thought for daily life is an occupational hazard. I have often been guilty of not making the connection between living and thinking as clear as might be done. I like to think systematically. I work out diagrams and think up categories in the effort to analyze and explain everything that is involved. Sometimes that procedure leads to abstractions, and abstractions may lose contact with the immediate, down-to-earth things of everyday life.

However, I am clear in my own mind that my personal thinking has grown fundamentally out of the attempt to make sense of life or, as Alfred North Whitehead says, "to elucidate immediate experience." I sometimes say to students, "If you keep pressing me on that question, I will start telling you about my childhood." That comment is meant with utmost seriousness. One of my teachers — H. Richard Niebuhr — said in class one day that the childhood of theologians is very important. That is certainly true of my own life.[5]

If you want to know what I believe about intercessory prayer, we have to begin when I was a child listening to my father praying in the woods at a time when he had been sick for a number of years. Healing was a long time coming, and it never came completely.

If you want to know why I think so much of life is ambiguous, we have to begin with my lying in bed at night hearing my parents argue and fight with each other. Both of them were good people who loved me very much. I could not understand why they could not get along with each other. The sinful, the tragic, and the demonic as well as the ambiguous all enter in when you think it all through.

If you want to know what I think about the demonic, we have to begin with my childhood when I begin to wonder why my friend Ben Crawford, Jr., who was black, walked to school, while I, a white child, rode a bus. None of the white adults around me, church members included, seemed to be bothered by this, even though the operating rule stated that schools were to be separate but equal. Everyone knew they were separate and unequal. They believed a lie and did not challenge each other with the plain truth. Only the demonic can account for that moral blindness.

If you want to know why I am liberal in my social, political, and economic thinking, we have to begin long ago when I was a teenager working in the textile mills in Griffin, Georgia. One day a stranger came walking through. He, it was said, was from the New York office of the company that partly owned the mill. I was told that this office was in the Empire State Building. Profits earned by the sweat of my parents, uncles, aunts, and cousins were being shipped off to New York to help pay for schools in New York — a rich state, while I attended a school in a poor county in Georgia. The South was a dependent region for a long time after the Civil War.

I could go on. However, I did not stop experiencing when I became an adult. If you want to know why I speak of the sinful, the tragic, the ambiguous, and the demonic, let me tell you about the experience of going through a divorce. Later on I will share more of the details of that long and painful struggle, but I can tell you that before it was through, I found it necessary to make use of all four categories. All of this was heightened by the fact that the divorce was liberating for me but destructive for my former wife. She never quite recovered, mainly because shortly after our separating, she developed cancer and eight years later died.

If you want to know why I believe in a limited, suffering, loving God who suffers with us in our pain and who forgives our sin, and who works with us to achieve the best possible outcome in every situation, then we will have to start with those experiences and many more I could name. Not only that, I have observed the world around me. I see suffering and tragedy. I see injustice. I see ambiguous moral situations in our political and economic life. I see the demonic working generation after generation to perpetuate misery and wrong. I cannot make sense out of my life nor out of what I see around me today or what I read about in the history books without reference to the sinful, the tragic, the demonic, and the ambiguous.

To me the connection between experience and thought, life and theology, is absolutely clear. Life and experience have to be interpreted. Interpretations can be wrong. I do not claim that my theology is right or true. I do insist that it was developed out of the honest and sincere effort to make sense out of life, to elucidate immediate experience, and to promote the art of living.

Everyone has a theology, if that means thinking about what Paul Tillich called "ultimate concern." We use ideas acquired over a lifetime to interpret our experience to find meaning and purpose in it all. Everybody tries to make sense out of life at some level. Implicit in such reflection is some conception of the ultimate nature of things, the way reality at its base is. Theology is the effort to think about issues of supreme significance in a more deliberate, systematic, and comprehensive fashion. Theologians are people who keep asking the childhood questions about existence. They spend most of their waking hours trying to think through what experience implies with reference to God and the ultimate questions of meaning, purpose, and duty.

I have struggled with the problem of evil and suffering as long as I can remember. Yet my own life, all things considered, has been almost uninterruptedly good. My question most often is, "Lord, why have so many good things happened to me, when others have known such tragedy?" I have had my own heartache and struggle. On one occasion years ago life seemed dark and hopeless. I can recall a few hours in deep despair when I came to know in my own heart how people could get desperate enough to take their own lives. That episode of hopelessness pales, however, in the face of all the good years and all the success and happiness I have known. Nevertheless, as a preacher and theologian, it is the quandary of evil and suffering that has concerned me over the years. I do not wish to immerse you in the endless debates of the theologians and philosophers who have wrestled with Job's predicament. No easy answer or set of propositions applies to all the miseries and injustices that plague the world. In the Bible many different things are said about suffering. Nowhere is there a systematic analysis of either its sources or its meaning. Life is complicated and multidimensional. Many things are true about our lives and our distress, but most of them are only partially true. What applies to some circumstances is not pertinent to others. Neither the Scriptures nor human reason gives us a satisfactory solution to all our questions.

I view the reflections to follow as an attempt to make sense out of life with respect to evil and suffering. The fundamental hope is that understanding may help to promote the art of life, to help us live well and to live better. In any case, I have intended to write an essay that would be credible in the presence of burning children. At the Murrah Federal Building in Oklahoma City on April 19, 1995, a deliberately planted bomb blew babies to bits in an instant, an act of evil that makes the words of the previous sentence almost too real to endure. As I wrote these words, divers were searching the bottom of the sea for human bodies and for wreckage of TWA flight 800 that exploded in mid-air shortly after take-off from New York City. It was not yet known whether the crash was an accident or the result of a terrorist act. Either way the problem of human agony is poignantly raised.

18

The exploration of suffering and evil begins in the next chapter with some necessary definitions and distinctions. After a chapter dealing with the meaning of human freedom and responsibility in relation to good and evil, three chapters set forth my understanding of sin, injustice and the demonic, the tragic, and the ambiguous. In Chapter Seven, I develop an understanding of a perfectly loving God who is limited in power but who works in all events to overcome evil and promote the highest possible good of all creatures. A final, more personal, chapter shows how events in my own life taught me more than any books I ever read the meaning of the many faces of evil.

---

1. "Cloud of Smoke, Pillar of Fire: Judaism, Christianity, and Modernity After the Holocaust," in *Auschwitz: Beginning of a New Era?*, ed. by Eva Fleischner (New York: KTAV Publishing House, Inc., 1977), 23. Quoted by John Roth in *Encountering Evil*, ed. by Stephen Davis (Atlanta: John Knox Press, 1981), 30.

2. Alfred North Whitehead, *Process and Reality*, ed. by David R. Griffin and Donald W. Sherburne (New York: The Free Press, 1978), 4.

3. Alfred North Whitehead, *The Function of Reason* (Boston: Beacon Press, 1958), 4.

4. *Ibid.*, 8.

5. I was fond of quoting Niebuhr to my classes with approval and then adding, "That is true of everybody except Hegel, who did not have a childhood. He just appeared one day in a classroom putting his elaborate philosophical system on the board!"

Chapter Two

Definitions And Distinctions:
Being Clear About What We Mean

He died all alone in a little cabin far removed from his family. It was not the way anybody wanted it, but Uncle Volney had smallpox. It happened nearly a hundred years ago. I heard the story from my grandmother. Volney Smith was her brother. The story of how he died while still quite a young man is one of those memories that connects me with the past. As Grandmother Martha Harris told it, people all around were dying, although some survived and took care of others. Uncle Volney was one of the unlucky ones. He was put off in a little cabin by himself. To reduce the danger of spreading the disease, his food was taken halfway from the kitchen to his cabin. He would come the rest of the way to get his meals when everyone had gone. One day he didn't come out. He died all alone, isolated from his family. Some men in the community who had survived the epidemic came to get his body. They put Uncle Volney in a wagon and took him to New Hope Baptist Church at midnight. They rang a bell all the way to warn those who had not had the disease to stay far away. They buried his body in the middle of the night. Once again he was alone in death as he had been at the end of his life.

The world is full of sad stories. Any week that passes will produce enough tragedy and heartbreak to keep the earth flooded with tears. Suffering goes on all around us all the time. As I was reviewing this section, a picture of a little four-year-old girl was

21

flashed on the television screen. A few days before, she had disappeared while riding her Big Wheel outside her home. The authorities then assumed she was abducted. Her distraught parents made a tearful plea to the kidnapper. The whole community had a broken heart, fearing that she has been harmed or killed. A family of four was brutally murdered in a nearby city. They were attacked, tortured, and killed in their own home by strangers who randomly chose their house. More than a dozen women in the Rochester, New York, area were murdered, nearly all involved in prostitution and connected with drugs. A young man went berserk in Canada and killed fourteen women on the campus of the University of Montreal. Having known much failure and rejection, he was full of hostility. He expressed it in one moment of violent madness that finally left him as well as his victims suddenly robbed of life.

A television show told the story of a young man in Chicago who had in desperation broken into the intensive care unit where his child was being kept alive by machines. He waved a gun to keep people away and pulled out the plugs. He held his son until he died. The child had swallowed a balloon and almost choked to death. His brain had been deprived of oxygen for a long time. He had no hope of ever being more than a vegetable. Doctors agreed that the infant would never be conscious again. The court refused permission to take away the technology that kept him breathing. The father out of love for the child and in desperation took extreme measures to relieve the suffering of all involved. Fortunately, a grand jury had the good sense not to indict him.

Seldom does a day pass but that we read newspaper accounts of people being killed or maimed by drunken drivers. A trial of a man took place in Kentucky who had, while intoxicated, run into a bus and killed 27 people. Hardly a more heart-wrenching sight can be imagined than a mother full of agony and anger telling how her teen-age daughter's life was taken in a crash caused by a driver stupid enough to drive a car while poisoned with alcohol. I can no longer laugh at impersonations of drunks with slurred speech.

In the summer of 1994 the weather news was dominated by the floods in Georgia, my home state. The home of my parents had a foot of water in every room, and they fared better than thousands whose homes had water to the rooftop, who had their farm land ruined, and all their possessions destroyed.

The list can be made as long as we want it to be. We have not mentioned the thousands of children at this moment dying of hunger, the homeless who roam the streets, the victims of cancer and AIDS and a hundred other diseases. There are the lonely, the despairing, the unloved, the unwanted, the mentally ill, and all the rest of those who suffer from the manifold ills to which this frail flesh of ours is heir. We only need mention Cambodia, Bosnia, Rwanda, and the Holocaust to summon up the horror of mass murder and genocide.

Accidents, disease, and violent crime come upon us without our consent. Disease strikes randomly without warning. Babies are born with congenital defects. Things can be going well, when an accident suddenly maims and mangles us for life. I had lived for fifty-eight years without ever having any of the predispositions toward or indications of heart disease. On November 30, 1988, however, I began to have chest pains about 9:00 p.m. on a Wednesday night. I spent eight days in Strong Memorial Hospital and came out with a fresh sense of the frailty and mortality of human flesh. We need not multiply examples. The fact and the mystery of suffering are all around us. Says Job in the midst of his misery, "I am not at ease; nor am I quiet; I have no rest; but trouble comes" (Job 3:26 RSV). Says the Psalmist, "I am weary with my crying; my throat is parched. My eyes grow dim with waiting for my God" (Psalm 69:3 RSV). These ancient cries are as modern as the computer on which I write these words. No fact of life raises more difficult problems for our Christian faith.

THE MEANING OF EVIL

Evil has many dimensions, and it is difficult to be precise, systematic, comprehensive, and consistent in the attempt to include all its facets and nuances of meaning. Its manifestations defy any simple or neat classifications, and one runs the danger of imposing categories arbitrarily in the quest for complete analysis, while the subtleties and complexities of actual life keep overflowing and frustrating the scheme. Despite these hazards I will offer some analysis and propose some classifications to give some order to our understanding, while attempting to qualify and complicate definitions as necessary in the quest of accuracy.

People use the term "evil" in two different ways. I learned this over many years of discussing the topic with seminary students and church people. **For some evil means moral or spiritual perversity.** It involves hatred and contempt for other people, wrongdoing, human volition, and bad intentions. Perverse motives and the desire to hurt, harm and destroy are evil in themselves. Evil is rape, murder, cruelty, injustice, kidnapping of children to abuse, torture and kill them. Suffering results in most if not all cases in some sense, but, strictly speaking, it is not the suffering as such that makes it evil in the primary sense. Evil always involves a distorted or perverse use of the powers of free moral beings expressed in bad motives and harmful actions. These beings may be human or superhuman, if one believes in a literal Satan. Evil can only be done by agents with powers of intelligence, intentionality, and choice. Suffering caused by illness, tornadoes, accidents, and other phenomena associated with nature or finitude are bad, awful, and lamentable but not evil in the strictest sense. No matter how great the disaster, loss, or misery to people and animals, events that do not involve moral agents intending or doing harm contain no evil in this way of thinking.

Others identify evil with suffering. Some pain and sorrow are caused by moral agents acting destructively. Other torments, tribulations, and frustrations are associated with our vulnerability as finite beings embedded in nature or with factors associated with the structure of reality. The suffering caused by cancer, hurricanes, earthquakes is evil, and the suffering is what constitutes the evil. Whatever its source, whether freedom or finitude, the identifying mark of evil is always suffering. If in a loose or extended sense, a tornado is said to be evil, the meaning is that it causes suffering, not that as an event in nature it is evil as such.

For the first group evil is moral perversity and is closely associated with suffering, but it is not the suffering that makes it evil but the spiritual wickedness. For the second group evil is suffering regardless of whether it is has its source in the nature of reality or in intelligent agents with free will. I belong to the second group. Whatever disrupts or destroys a potential for enjoyment and thus produces anguish in experiencing subjects whether human or animal, I call evil regardless of the cause, context, or circumstance. Neither way of defining evil is right, making the other wrong. It is important for purposes of communication and understanding, however, that we know how a given person employs the term. With this clarification, we may proceed toward more precise and systematic definitions of evil, but first an important question must be answered.

Can there be evil that involves no suffering? I have so far denied this possibility. However, some might argue that bad intentions and wicked thoughts are evil in themselves, although the person who harbored them does no actual harm to anyone else. Suppose Arthur is resentful of Sam for some reason and secretly hopes that something awful will happen to him. Further imagine that Arthur never does anything at all to bring his hope to fulfillment but nurtures his hate and hostility in the privacy of his own heart. I contend that Arthur suffers from his own wicked thoughts and bad motives. A potential for enjoyment that comes from mutual respect and affection is being frustrated. We may speculate about the damage that festering malice and enmity might eventually cause to his body, but we can be sure that his spirit is sick already. It is difficult to imagine that such internal distress will not eventually affect and do harm to other people to some degree. Even if he feels perverse pleasure in his animosity, a more profound joy is being missed. Healthy enjoyment comes from being rightly related to God and others in thought and deed. Moreover, I would insist that God is offended and suffers from Arthur's malice. I have difficulty thinking that hate can be entirely harmless. However, if it can be shown that no harm of any sort is associated with Arthur's inner spite, either to him, to God, or to others, I would have to say no evil is present. If someone insists that Arthur's spiritual perversity is evil in itself independently of whether suffering is involved, I will not argue with that preference of definition. Nevertheless, I hold that spiritual perversity always involves suffering, and it is the suffering that makes it evil.

THE BASIC DEFINITION

Objectively, evil is the disruption or destruction of a potential for enjoyment. Enjoyment means the satisfaction felt as the accompaniment of the objective actualization of the good.[1] **Subjectively**, evil is experienced as suffering. By suffering is meant the anguish accompanying the blockage or frustration of a potential for enjoyment. In human beings suffering may be physical, mental, or spiritual. The varieties of enjoyment are many and thus are the forms of misery. Physical pain, diseases that destroy body and mind, being unloved or unwanted, loneliness, not belonging, having no home, hunger, abject poverty and want, failure in the pursuit of desirable goals, meaninglessness, injustice, despair, premature death — these indicate but do not exhaust the forms of torment to which we are heir in this sometimes terrible world.

Suffering in the broad sense is not restricted to human beings but applies to animals as well, i.e., all sentient beings. Any organism capable of feeling and experiencing can suffer. While the focus here is on human suffering, let it be said plainly that animal pain is evil.

STRONG AND SHADOW DIMENSIONS

Evil includes not only a *strong aspect* whereby some structured potential for good already in existence is frustrated, disrupted, or destroyed but also refers to a *shadow side* comprising the good that is missed.[2] The latter is the joy, the success, the satisfactions, the happiness, the loving relationships that never came to pass because the requisite conditions were not present or because calamity struck. It is the absence of the good that might have been but was not, and we suffer from that. The shadow dimension of evil is the failure to achieve the finest that could have occurred within some appropriate frame of reference.[3]

The strong dimension of evil is usually what we have in mind. Evil in the primary sense refers to the partial ruination or total annihilation of a given potential for healthy or just enjoyment. The evils that break our hearts are those real and present instances of misery and affliction that threaten or shatter the pleasure of living — raging famine, ravaging illness, devastating accidents,

26

uncaring cruelty to people and animals, natural disasters that waste life and property, senseless abduction and murder of children, brutal torture of political enemies, hatred and violence toward racial, sexual, and ethnic minorities, vicious subjugation of the helpless, and the like.

STRUCTURAL FACTORS

It is important to note some constituent factors within the nature of things that are essential to understanding the possibility and fact of evil. Some are intrinsic to the nature of reality and so have metaphysical status. Most important of all in this connection, finitude implies vulnerability to disruption and destruction. This fact underlies all actual and potential suffering. The correlation of finitude and susceptibility to suffering is inescapable.

Another metaphysical correlation means that there cannot be a world in which good things can happen without the possibility of bad things happening. We cannot have one without the other. This is part of the meaning of ambiguity. The very principles and processes that produce pleasure and happiness when they work properly produce misery when things go wrong. The digestive system is constructed to give us satisfaction when we eat good food. It follows that we can get a stomach ache if something upsets normal functioning.

Moreover, the more good that is possible, the more suffering is possible. It is impossible to increase the capacity for experiencing broader ranges and depths of enjoyment without simultaneously creating the capacity for greater misery and failure. Worms know neither the heights of human joy nor the depths of human anguish. The fact that human beings can experience meaning and purpose that give us happiness means that we can also experience despair and hopelessness that make life awful. The same capacities that make human enjoyment possible make possible human suffering. We cannot have one without the other.

Again, notice that complicated things are easy to break down. Consider the human brain. The complexity of this system of cells and connections is mind-boggling. It is this intricate arrangement of tissue that makes possible thought, love, choice, and all that makes human life distinctive. Yet this same complexity makes it very vulnerable. It seems inescapable that the more good a living being can experience, the more complex it must be, the more evil it can suffer, and the more vulnerable it is. Much more can go wrong with a human brain than with a mountain, and it is much easier to destroy.

In all the above examples the connections mentioned refer to possibilities and capacities. They do not involve necessary or inevitable evil, although the probabilities are very high that evil will occur. Nevertheless, if the best that is possible occurs always, no actual evil emerges.[4] Something must go wrong to produce real suffering. Beyond this, however, are certain necessities, correlations, laws, and limitations within the structure of finite reality that frustrate the achievement of an ideal or perfect good that can be imagined but may not be possible in certain situations that arise factually. Because of these structural factors, suffering cannot always be avoided even when the best that can be done is done. Even when nothing has gone wrong, evil may be present. Prominent here is the inescapable presence of moral ambiguity in many situations.

In some cases, neither divorce nor continuing the marriage offers anything but deep suffering for the couple and their children. The only choice is the lesser of two evils or the better of two ambiguous goods. A soldier who rightfully kills an enemy in a just war causes suffering in doing what is morally required. So does a police officer who tragically has to shoot a crazed person as the only way to prevent him or her from murdering a half-dozen hostages cornered in a fast food restaurant.

On the one hand, capitalism as a system exalts individual freedom, distributes economic power, and generates wealth. On the other hand, it leads to considerable inequalities and the concentration of wealth in private hands. Most often this power is used to perpetuate privilege originally acquired by some combination of vigorous enterprise, good luck, fortunate circumstances, merit, and ruthlessness. It may be impossible to correct some of the faults and limitations of capitalism without losing some of the values or introducing new evils and ambiguities. Good and evil

28

are to this extent inseparable twins, like the wheat and the tares in the story Jesus told. A social policy can be just in the sense of embodying the best available trade-off or compromise between competing values and yet involve a mixture of good and evil that cannot be disentangled. No matter what is done, some will be injured. The tragic is the accompaniment of this kind of ambiguity. Inevitably some people will be hurt, while others be protected from harm or enabled to achieve legitimate aspirations by the same deed.

Some affirmative action policies may enable groups who have been previously excluded from educational opportunities or jobs to catch up but only at the cost of penalizing individuals of the formerly privileged group who themselves have not discriminated against anyone and who deserve a equal chance with others for particular positions. Justified abortions may involve both tragedy and moral ambiguity. Freedom and equality may be so correlated in some but not necessarily all situations that increasing one decreases the other. Sometimes justice can be achieved only through violence, and at other times the price of peace may be continuing injustice. Values may be in conflict, and in some cases no possible resolution can separate out the good and preserve it while eliminating all the evil. This is a feature of the very nature of reality that cannot be transcended. Nevertheless, we can envision a perfect or ideal situation or outcome even though it is impossible to attain. We can imagine a just situation that does good to all and harms no one, although in actual practice, this ideal outcome cannot always be achieved because ambiguity attaches to every conceivable solution.

These incompatibilities and correlations within reality cannot be avoided. This list of possible complexities and frustrations that cannot be avoided goes further still. Not all just and good aims of individuals are possible of realization, since the achievement of some necessarily rules out others. One good choice may of necessity eliminate the possibility of other equally good but different choices. A person with enough native talent to be both the foremost cancer researcher of the time and the world's greatest poet cannot realize both goals without limiting either.

Some frustrations have to do with the nature of time and space. Not all passionate music lovers can be physically present for the last concert of a world-renowned pianist who is retiring upon the fiftieth anniversary of his professional career.[5] Time moves forward in a one-way trajectory so that we cannot go back to correct a foolish or careless mistake that will have deleterious even devastating effects for the rest of our lives.

I have mentioned the following structural factors associated with the fact and possibility of evil: (1) the inseparable connection between finitude and vulnerability, (2) the correlation of possibilities of good with possibilities of evil, (3) the correlation between increasing the potential for good and increasing the potential for evil, (4) the connection between increasing complexity and increasing vulnerability, (5) situational ambiguity involving an inseparable mixture of good and evil, (6) the mutual exclusiveness of some values and choices with others, and (7) the limitations associated with time and space. Obviously, some evils or potential evils entailed by these structural factors are more significant and more heartbreaking than others. There may be others not listed here.

Whether God could have created a world in which only the good and the potential for increasing good existed without any potential for evil is a highly speculative question difficult to answer. Presumably a miracle-working God who constantly intervened to manipulate outcomes could prevent most particular instances of physical suffering. Otherwise, finitude and vulnerability to harm do appear to be necessarily correlated. However, it would appear that not even God could always separate the intertwining of good and evil in some cases of moral ambiguity. A similar question is whether a world with no suffering at all would be desirable. If possible but not desirable, that itself is a metaphysical limitation. If the best of all possible worlds is one in which suffering is unavoidable or desirable, that is a tragic situation involving God as well as us.

MORAL EVIL AND NATURAL EVIL

Evil experienced as suffering takes two forms: **moral evil** and **natural evil**. **Moral evil** is the possibility inherent in freedom.

Natural evil is the possibility inherent in finitude.[6] From freedom springs the suffering associated with sin, injustice, and the demonic. From finitude arises the suffering associated with the tragic quality of life, moral ambiguity, and unavoidable ignorance.

Moral evil refers to the suffering caused by human irresponsibility, i.e., sin.[7] Under sin is included deliberate action that is intended to harm or that is done despite the fact that it does harm. Also embraced is non-intentional harm that is done resulting from carelessness. We are responsible for misery caused by avoidable ignorance and for harmful acts that could have been prevented by using our abilities intelligently and prudently. The driver who, while intoxicated or because of failure to exercise due caution in backing out of a driveway, non-intentionally kills a child is guilty of wrongdoing.[8]

To speak of **moral evil**, then, is to say that much of the suffering in the world is caused by what people deliberately or carelessly do to each other. We bring a lot of misery on ourselves by our foolishness, our negligence, and our selfishness. Murders, cruelty, crime, and all sorts of meanness and injustice are committed by people out of fear, hate, and greed. Drunken drivers who kill and maim are abusing their freedom, however much they may be suffering from a disease. We hurt ourselves, and people hurt each other by their acts, attitudes, and choices.

Under **natural evil** is included the suffering arising from factors in the nature of things and the things of nature that involve no human irresponsibility. Harm may be done and suffering caused where none was intended and where unavoidable ignorance was present. Accidents involving no human irresponsibility may produce suffering but involve no sin. In addition, the usual list of natural evils includes the physical pain and emotional distress associated with disease, injury, and bodies badly deformed or disabled. Floods, storms, earthquakes, lightning, and the like are natural evils in so far as they cause suffering to people and animals.

The very nature of reality makes it highly probable that accidents, diseases, and destruction will sometimes occur. Atoms, molecules, stones, trees, animals, and people all have parts arranged in a certain way that make them what they are. If this organization is disturbed, destruction occurs. This means everything finite is vulnerable, fragile, and subject to disruption. This is closely related to the fact that we live in an interdependent, law-abiding world in which a plurality of chains of causation or activity are present. Things interact with good and bad effects. They may collide or interfere with each other. Destruction may result. Accidents happen. Things collide, break, fall apart, blow up, erode, rust, and rot. If we are talking about living organisms, disorganization among their parts causes pain and eventually death. Suffering related to **natural evils** of this type is a disturbance of healthy functioning in the body or mind of a living being. Human and animal bodies get sick and die. They are mangled and destroyed by stones, bullets, storms, earthquakes, and other devastations too numerous to list. It may be that any real world worth living in will be like this. It is hard to conceive of free, interacting finite beings that are not vulnerable. We are flesh. We bleed, hurt, suffer, and die.

Any specific **natural evil**, however, that involves harm to our bodies is in principle avoidable in that it does not follow from any necessity or law of reality as such. However, the occurrence of **natural evil** in general is not only highly probable but abounds in fact all around us every day. It exemplifies laws, patterns, and processes built into the nature of things, but no particular event involving bodily harm in which it occurs is necessitated by them. Something must go wrong in actual fact that could have gone right for these **natural evils** to ensue. Every specific incident of this type is a contingent event not a necessary one. The laws of physics and biology always hold in an automobile accident that kills people, but they do not mandate that accidents occur.

Other forms of **natural evil** are different in this respect. Some suffering, we have noted, results from structural factors that are built into the nature of reality. This is **natural evil**, since no human irresponsibility is involved. In some situations even the best that can be done will unavoidably produce some suffering in the very attempt to do only good. This is why I make so much of the fact of moral ambiguity.

Obviously, some suffering arises from a mixture of human irresponsibility (freedom) and non-human factors (nature). People who knowingly build houses over a geological fault with a high probability for producing earthquakes in the near future participate in their calamity in ways that those who build there in innocent ignorance are not. The line between what involves human irresponsibility and what does not may be hard to draw in fact in many instances, although we do so readily in principle. Moreover, let us note that **moral evil** springing from irresponsible freedom presupposes finitude and its imbeddedness in nature. It is only because we are finite and vulnerable that human agents by their irresponsibility can inflict suffering on themselves or others.

The distinction between **natural** and **moral evil** is variously made. For John Hick the difference is in the agency involved. **Natural evil** is produced by non-human agents and **moral evil** by human agents.[9] For David Griffin, the difference is between suffering intended (**moral evil**) and suffering undergone, regardless of the agent (**natural evil**).[10] I prefer my distinction since it deals better with the in-between category of accidents, that may or may not be caused by human carelessness. Suppose a person who was exercising due caution hit and killed a child who suddenly darted out in the street right in front of him. Unlike Hick, I would not call accidental harm done by a person who was not irresponsible in the situation **moral evil**. Suppose the driver was not paying attention and hit the child unintentionally when due caution would have prevented the accident. Unlike Griffin, I would call unintended harm done to another by a person who was acting carelessly **moral evil**.

THE RELATIONSHIP
BETWEEN SUFFERING AND EVIL

The relationship between suffering and evil is complex.[11] In this connection, some make a distinction between **genuine** and **apparent evil**.[12] For David Griffin, e.g., **genuine evil** is suffering that is pointless, destructive, unnecessary, and leads to no compensating good. The world would have been better off without it, all things considered. **Apparent evil** is suffering that eventuates in or is the means to a larger good or is compensated for in some larger context.[13] Before the invention of anesthesia, the amputation of a gangrenous leg to save a life would by this definition be an apparent evil. Here I object. While there is a compensating good, the pain is excruciating, and the screams are real. Hence, the designation of this event as an "apparent" evil trivializes the intense suffering associated with it.

I prefer to distinguish between absolute evil and relative evil.[14] **Absolute evil** is suffering that is pointless, unnecessary, purely destructive with no redeeming elements or outcomes for anyone ever. **Relative evil** is suffering that is partially, wholly, or more than compensated for in some larger context or in the long run. The connections of suffering and evil to some compensating or justifying good are multifarious. Consider the following list that, by and large, runs from unqualified (absolute) evil to suffering that is so trivial as to be insignificant (degrees of relative evil).

1. **Events that are totally pointless, destructive, unredeemed, and unnecessary:** the torture and eventual murder of a child by a parent that has only negative effects on all touched by it over a long period of time.

2. **The involuntary suffering of some that leads to an immense good for others:** a minor earthquake that kills hundreds leading to precautions that later save thousands of lives in a major tremor.

3. **Evil acts that have unintended consequences for good in the long run:** Joseph's being sold into slavery by his brothers becoming the means by which he later saved his family from famine (Genesis 45).

4. **Deliberate harm or violence done to a person or group in order to prevent or overcome a larger moral evil:** a policeman who finds a brief but opportune moment to kill a crazed gunman systematically murdering a group of hostages in a bank. Consider also participants in a justified war who kill the enemy as a last resort to overcome cruel tyranny and oppression and to achieve greater justice when all non-violent attempts have failed.

5. **Voluntary suffering that benefits others:** a person who volunteers to undergo medical experimentation that kills him/her but leads to the discovery of a drug that saves thousands of lives. Christians will also think of Jesus and his path to the cross.

6. **Suffering that leads to moral and spiritual maturity hardly imaginable otherwise:** a man who loses an arm to cancer testifying that he would not have it back if he could because the experience taught him so much about life and love that he never knew before.

7. **Pain that is avoidable, voluntary, and temporary, endured for the sake of some personal goal:** the agony of a marathon runner after twenty-five miles who could stop any time she/he chooses.

This list could be indefinitely extended, but it serves to illustrate the complexity of the situation. Three factors can be noted that enter into the relativizing of evil.

a. Is the suffering a necessary and unavoidable means to the eventual larger good, or is some other path to the same goal available with less or no suffering?

b. Is the suffering experienced by the same individual, group, or generation that is compensated, or do some suffer while others reap the benefits?

c. Is the suffering voluntary or involuntary?

The more the first alternative in each pair prevails, the more relative is the evil involved. Obviously, in specific cases it is not possible or easy to measure the exact relativity of evils or to designate some as purely and simply absolute without qualification.

Evils, whether absolute or relative, vary in kind (physical or psychic) and severity (massiveness, intensity, duration, numbers of people involved, etc.). Some relative evils may be comparatively worse than some absolute evils. For example, the agonizing amputation of a leg without anesthesia is greater in intensity although it saves a life (relative evil) than a mild cold which does no one any good whatsoever now or later (absolute evil). All suffering is relatively evil, however, even when it is a necessary means to some desired and worthy gain that justifies it. This is another dimension of the fact that the world contains a tragic element. It would be better if the highest ends of life could be achieved by sufficiently stern challenges that did not require excruciating pain and heartbreaking misery.

35

GOD'S RESPONSIBILITY FOR EVIL

Is God responsible for evil? By the nature of the case, we have to say that God is indirectly responsible for evil. This follows from the fact that God created the world. If there were no world, there would be no evil. Therefore, at least we have to say that God is *directly* responsible for the world and *indirectly* responsible for any evil that occurs in the world.

But is God ever *directly* responsible for evil? Does God ever cause evil? Surprisingly enough, there are a few passages in the Bible that teach this. Consider Isaiah 45:7:

> *I form light and create darkness, I make weal and create woe. I am the Lord, who does all these things* (RSV).

This verse occurs in a larger passage that stresses the sovereignty of God. God is the Creator who rules everything. God is the Almighty before whom the nations are as a drop from a bucket. If you emphasize the power of God and the sovereignty of God and stress it strongly enough, that leads toward the conclusion that God does everything. There is no power but God. God's agency is the only agency. Anything that is done is done by God.

The same holds in Christian history. Those theologians who have stressed the sovereignty of God the strongest end up by saying that God is the cause of everything, including what we call evil. John Calvin in the 16th century taught an extreme doctrine in this regard. God makes every event happen just as it does without any exception. Nevertheless, Calvin insists on two further points. (1) We are responsible for the evil that we do. When we sin, we are held accountable, because we did it and we did it voluntarily. We wanted to sin. It expresses our character and intent. This is true, even if at another and deeper level God is the cause of our action. A good analogy would be the actions of the characters in a novel in relation to the author. The butler in the mystery story committed the murder of his own volition out of motives that are quite clear. Yet at another level it is the author of the book who makes the butler do it. So it is with our deeds in relation to God as the ultimate determiner of all that occurs. (2) We cannot call God evil, even

36

when God causes pain and suffering. By definition right is what God does, and God's deeds always serve a good and worthy purpose known mostly only to God. Hence, we have to speak paradoxically when we speak of God's responsibility for evil. It is both true in one sense and not true in another sense.

My own view is very different. I do not believe that God directly causes particular instances of suffering. God does not make specific evil things happen for some reason. If we ask whether God wills this or that instance of suffering in an immediate way, the answer must be NO. Some passages of scripture teach otherwise, of course. I do not believe we ought to see things this way today. God is ultimately responsible for the *possibility* of bad things happening, since God made the world. But God does not cause each instance of suffering for a particular purpose.

Rather, when accident, disease, and violence bring great pain and misery to us, I believe that God's heart is broken like ours. God feels our pain and suffers our agony with us. Only if this is so can I believe that God is truly full of love and compassion. Yet in our sorrow God and we can make the best of it from now on to bring new life and enjoyment out of the broken pieces. God uses every event, good and bad, as an opportunity to work in us and through us and in all things to bring the greatest possible happiness, joy, and love into being. In that fact we can trust. So believing, we can try to attune our lives to that saving purpose, knowing that nothing can separate us from the love of God.

---

1. Enjoyment here has a Whiteheadian meaning. Organisms are driven by *eros* to fulfill their craving for the good. The good and the process of achieving it are experienced as enjoyment. Only those enjoyments that are healthy and just are morally licit, i.e., those that promote the optimum freedom, equality, and happiness of all individuals and communities. The ethical-spiritual norm is this: Maximize maximizing enjoyments. This means we should seek those enjoyments that most fittingly unite with other enjoyments into ever enlarging networks of harmonious and mutually sustaining activities that increase pleasure, meaning, purpose, and well-being. God is the All-Embracing Individual-Social Organism whose purpose is the fulfillment of the just aims

of all organisms (including the Divine Organism). This is a philosophical translation of the Great Commandments of Jesus to love God with our whole beings and our neighbors as we love ourselves. For a development of these ideas, see "enjoyment" in the index of most of my books published since 1969.

2. Some of the material in this section has been taken from my *Theological Biology: The Case for a New Modernism* (Lewiston, NY: The Edwin Mellen Press, 1991), 254-263. Considerable revision in the definition of concepts and in wording has taken place.

3. Obviously, some limits have to be drawn and some appropriate framework assumed. A child starving to death in a severe widespread famine might be better off today if some more favorable set of possible events in the indefinite past had occurred instead of what did happen. Eventually we are pushed back to the origin of the world and to the ultimate causative factors that generated just this kind of world and established the determining conditions that set in motion some set of contingent events leading to the present and to the child's birth. Any number of things could have been different along the way that would have made the present situation more promising. The evils that disturb us most are the events that represent a worse rather than a better outcome within some circumscribed set of real potentials more or less nearby in time and space to a given outcome.

4. This is a subtle and difficult point. Here I refer to what is ideally possible before anything has gone wrong. Under some factual circumstances, of course, no matter what we do some suffering will occur. For example, if the spinal cord of a person remains intact and healthy until that person dies, no evil occurs in that respect. This is an example of what I am referring to. However, if an accident occurs and severs the spinal cord, that person may undergo lifelong suffering no matter what is done at that point, given the present state of medical knowledge and technology.

5. In today's comic strip (July 9, 1996) Hagar noted this in frustration when he observed that it was impossible for him to be in three places at once. It seems the Liars, Loafers, and Beer Drinking Clubs were meeting the same night.

6. "Physical evil is the natural implication of creaturely finitude. Moral evil is the tragic implication of creaturely freedom." Paul Tillich, *Systematic Theology*, 3 vols. (Chicago: University of Chicago Press, 1951, 1957, 1963), I:269. I prefer to speak of the possibility inherent in finitude and freedom, since Tillich's formulation suggests a structural inevitability that is universal though not ontologically necessary since it occurs in freedom. This

Augustinian paradox that combines freedom with universality never quite escapes contradiction in my view, despite his and Reinhold Niebuhr's different ways of either denying logical absurdity (Tillich) or living with it by making a distinction between thought in which Aristotelian logic holds and experience in which it does not (Niebuhr). These subtle issues will be discussed in more detail in the chapter on sin.

7. Sin, of course, also has a religious meaning in which it refers to estrangement from God, rebellion against God, and the like. Here I deal with the moral dimension of sin, i.e., acts that do harm to people.

8. We do not normally associate freedom of choice with animals, but the line between instinctual behavior in animals and intentional action in humans to harm or help another being may not be as sharp, as absolute, or as easily drawn as we might initially assume. The question as to whether some higher animals act deliberately with at least a dim awareness of intended consequences and hence are in a limited sense free will have to be left unresolved here.

9. See *Evil and the God of Love* (San Francisco: Harper & Row, 1978), 12.

10. See *God, Power and Evil* (Philadelphia: Westminster Press, 1976), 27-28.

11. The material in this section has been taken from my *Theological Biology*, 257-259.

12. See David Griffin, *God, Power and Evil*, 22.

13. See the discussion between Griffin and Hick on this point in *Encountering Evil*, ed. by Stephen Davis (Atlanta: John Knox Press, 1981), 103-104, 122-123, 129.

14. The distinction between absolute and relative evil makes it possible to accommodate those who want to say that some events are both genuinely evil and that they will or can be compensated or more than compensated for by their contribution or association with some larger eventual good. David Griffin and John Hick argue inconclusively over what is genuinely evil and what is merely apparently so. The distinction between absolute and relative evil may allow both to have their point but in a less confusing or paradoxical way. See their exchange in *Encountering Evil*, 103-104, 122-123, 129.

Chapter Three

The Meaning Of Freedom:
Could We Do Better If Only We Would?

She was only sixteen years old when the court sentenced her to death for her crime. She and two or three other teen-age girls had attacked and killed an old woman. They broke into her house. They kicked, stabbed, and beat her viciously and without mercy until she died. As I listened to the story, I felt a growing rage within me. How could anyone be so cruel, so insensitive, so callous, and so mean? How could they listen to her pleas for mercy and not be touched? They set upon the old woman who had done nothing to them and assaulted her body until she fell to the floor. The poor soul died repeating the Lord's Prayer. The ringleader of the group was fifteen years old at the time. She was caught, tried, found guilty, and sentenced to die. As I heard the story — let me be candid — I was so angry with her despite her youth that I almost wanted to strangle her myself. The premeditated viciousness and cruelty were totally unprovoked and without cause. I felt all my convictions against the death penalty being tested. Are there not some crimes so monstrous that those who commit them forfeit their membership in the human community? I was outraged and wrathful that these heartless girls could continue to stab and beat an old woman who was pleading for mercy and praying to God.

A few minutes later I was watching this young woman being interviewed. First of all, it was the look on her face that got to me. It was an expression of such sadness and tragedy that, despite what she had done, I felt my heart softening a bit. She said she didn't want to die. She wanted to live out her normal span of years. She began to tell the story of her own life. She had been mistreated and abused in her own home. She spoke of how ashamed she was of her family situation. They seemed different somehow. Here was a vulnerable, sensitive child who needed love and security in her own tender years and had not received it. I sat there watching her and listening. The sorrow and pain on her face broke through my rage. A large tear formed in each eye and slowly ran down her cheek.

What inner pain and humiliation she must have known in her early years. It all came to the surface now and was plainly revealed in the expression on her face. She had done a vicious thing and had been sentenced to die for it. Her young life appeared to be headed for a tragic end. She had never known how good life can be when you are loved and cared for by those who matter most. I shall never forget the look on her face. A few minutes ago, I had been ready to strangle her. Now I was moved to tears of my own and wanted to reach out in compassion and let her know that somebody cares. There but for the grace of God and love of family and friends — especially in those early years — go we all.

It was a rather remarkable experience for me. I went from wrath and rage to mercy and compassion toward one human being. She was a cruel murderer. She was also a precious young life whose own spirit had been crushed by people and powers beyond her control when she needed to be loved and nourished.

ARE WE RESPONSIBLE?

A lot of questions are raised by this sad story. There is, for example, the terribly difficult question of how free and responsible we are for our actions. Every fiber of my being wants to say that we are accountable for what we do, no matter what our childhood was like. But I am not sure that in every instance we have the power to choose otherwise than we do. Just as a bridge can hold up only so much weight, maybe our human frame can bear only so much and beyond that collapses into actions that are beyond our control. A few tragic souls may have become so broken down by their past that they have lost most of their capacity to decide between good and evil. They may be nearly enslaved to the demons that rage within. In any case, I am pretty sure that some people have a greater range of choice than others.

One thing has impressed me. Again and again when the newspapers report some horrible crime that is truly outrageous, the follow-up articles on the childhood backgrounds reveal a similar pattern. Time after time it turns out that these violent people have themselves been victims of violence. Parents who mistreat their children have often themselves been abused. Assassins and murderers have frequently known childhood experiences in which they were beaten or neglected or felt themselves deeply humiliated and unloved. I state no universal law, no necessary connection between past history and present wrongdoing, but the link must be taken into account as a factor that conditions free choice.

Recently the courts have highlighted the issue.[1] Moosa Hanoukai beat his wife to death with a wrench. His attorney argued that Manijeh Hanoukai had psychologically emasculated her husband by making him sleep on the floor, calling him names, and paying him meager wages. As a result he lost all self-esteem. He was a Persian Jew and thus prevented from seeking a divorce. The jury acquitted him of murder but convicted him of manslaughter.

Erik and Lyle Menendez killed their parents with shotguns. The juries who heard their cases deadlocked. Attorneys argued that the brothers had been subjected to years of psychological and sexual abuse that finally drove them to extreme measures. In their retrial, they were both found guilty.

Daimion Osby killed two unarmed men. He won a mistrial after his lawyers argued that he lived in a racist country and that his life in the inner-city caused him to suffer from "urban survival syndrome," a malady that convinced him that he had no alternative except killing.

Lorena Bobbitt cut off her husband's penis with a kitchen knife. She was acquitted of malicious wounding by reason of temporary insanity. She claimed that her husband had abused her for years, had tried to rape her, and then passed out drunk.

Anne Blackburn shot her husband to death. In her first trial the jury deadlocked 11-1 in her favor. On retrial she was acquitted on the basis of a battered woman defense.

Are we always responsible for what we do? How free are we? Could we do otherwise than we do? How are choices actually made? What can be said in a more systematic way?

THE PRESUPPOSITION OF FREEDOM

Before getting into the question of what actually determines which choices are made, it must be said that the necessary presupposition of the kind of freedom human beings have is the capacity for self-transcendence, which can be taken as a definition of spirit.[2] The self has the ability as subject to stand back from the world and from itself and to examine them as objects. From that vantage point the self as subject — the "I" that is the examining agent — can observe what is factually the case and imagine alternative possibilities. In the capacity to entertain the contrast between what is and what might be lies the possibility of creative self-guidance and self-transformation. It enables us to set goals and to devise means to reach them.

The highest reach of self-transcendence is the capability of the self as subject (the "I" self) to inspect the self as object (the "it" self). In this posture we can inspect what is going on in us internally. We can observe, contemplate, analyze, organize, evaluate, interpret, and otherwise engage the self in conversation, questioning, and debate. Above all, we can consider alternative possibilities of self-activity — thinking, acting, feeling, and the like. We can even catch ourselves in the act of self-examining the self, so that the self as subject is now at another level observing as object the self as subject observing the self as object. This self-reflexive activity can proceed until our mental powers have exhausted their capacity to hold in view all the ascending levels of observing the self as observer of the observer. But at whatever level, the self as subject is always the examiner and never the examined. The "I" can never look the "I" in the "eye" any more than the eye can look itself in the eye directly, i.e., without the aid of a mirror.

An example may help. When I was a young pastor right out of seminary, I was visiting a church member in the hospital. At some point while continuing to talk to her, I mentally stepped back and began to peruse the scene. I observed what she was saying and what I was saying in reply and wondered if I were doing it right. I was trying to remember what the pastoral theology books said to do next, musing that "Well, here I am doing what I have been trained to do, and am I feeling inadequate and insecure!" Then I became aware of what I was doing, that I was standing back watching myself in action. There I was momentarily watching myself watching myself. Fortunately, at that juncture, I settled back into the normal mode of operation; otherwise, I would have lost my place in the conversation.

In short, the self's capacity to make itself and the world an object and to contrast what is with what might be is the necessary presupposition of the distinctive human capacity for choice. Beyond this, it may be useful to borrow a set of terms from Paul Tillich to provide a framework for discussion. He speaks of the interdependence of freedom and destiny.[3] These polar elements are together in every situation of choice. Destiny is the formed genetic-social-individualized structure within which freedom as the power of creative self-direction is exercised. My destiny is myself as given — constructed by my biological endowment, my cultural inheritance, my life history, and my own past decisions. "Destiny is not a strange power which determines what shall happen to me. It is myself as given, formed by nature, history, and myself. My destiny is the basis of my freedom; my freedom participates in shaping my destiny."[4] My destiny was and is to be a white, male, Baptist, southern, American Christian with certain natural endowments of intellect, talent, and predisposition, born in Georgia to J. W. and Beulah Cauthen as an only child who grew up among farmers and mill workers during and following the great depression of the 1930s and who has come to have a particular set of beliefs, attitudes, value commitments, and habits of feeling. My freedom is a dynamic element exercised within the structure formed by that destiny. The union of my freedom with my destiny creates the content and direction of my life. Destiny guides my freedom. Freedom helps to shape my destiny.

THE MEANING OF FREEDOM

Freedom is most often discussed as if it were a generic capacity possessed in full and equally by everyone. It is said that human beings have "free will," as if this were some uniform power to choose present in all people independently of any and all circumstances. The assumption, if unqualified, is that in any given moment confronted with two alternatives we could with ease or great effort elect either one by just deciding to do so. The implication for morality is that everyone could do right and avoid wrong if only she or he would in any situation. Let us concede at once that we are more likely to magnify freedom when we speak of our enemies. We are inclined to assume that their wrongdoing is sheer perversity uncomplicated by circumstance and lacking ambiguity. We more readily understand that we and those we defend are caught up in a maelstrom of constraining conditions so acute that our misdeeds are rendered almost innocent! We do not often make these assumptions as explicitly as I have done. Nevertheless, my impression is that we are often unguarded in the way we speak of freedom and at least appear to assume that people could in every case do better or at least differently if only they would. It is perhaps practically necessary and partly true to think this way, but the whole truth I suspect is much more complicated than this.

By freedom in the most general sense, I mean the ability to choose among alternatives, i.e., to enact one option rather than another. In this broad sense, freedom is possessed by animals as well as people. With two bowls of food before them, dogs can certainly pick the more appealing one. The ability to decide among options, preferring some to others, is a general power that can function at an indefinite number of levels.[5] In people, however, choice involves the capacity to analyze problems, imagine and evaluate options, and after due deliberation to choose among alternatives. Freedom in the peculiar human sense means creative self-determination. Choice is determined by the self in its totality as directed by its own goals, obligations, norms, attitudes, beliefs, and values. Any particular decision expresses the whole self as it has come to be what it is at that moment.

46

This view stands between and rejects both extreme indeterminism and extreme determinism. Extreme indeterminism denies all determination by factors within or without the self. Every act is purely contingent, depending on the mere arbitrary choice of the self, unconditioned by anything, motivated, governed, and directed by nothing. The self chooses to choose what it chooses by just choosing at the moment in particular circumstance. Extreme determinism asserts complete determination of every act by powers and influences that dictate outcomes without deviation. The self has no independent or autonomous agency but is merely the register and instrument of causes over which it has no control.[6] As long as these are the alternatives, determinism will nearly always win the argument. A totally unmotivated, unguided act makes no sense rationally and is untrue to our experience. Beyond indeterminism and determinism is self-determinism. Self-determinism rejects both the absolute necessity imposed on the self from without in determinism and the absolute contingency of choice unguided by motives within the self in indeterminism. The self is the cause of its own choices and actions, indetermined externally but determined internally by its own purposes and norms.

We need a view that neither exaggerates nor underestimates freedom. More specifically, it is important to understand exactly what freedom is and how choice functions in human beings. Two distinct categories are required for understanding, but in practice they flow into each other.

1. **Normal Choice**. From day to day our choices are governed by our formed character. By character I mean the total constellation of habits, motivations, values, aims, attitudes, beliefs, tastes, emotional patterns, moral commitments, genetic-biological make-up, psychic cravings, and so on that constitute the predisposition to act in certain ways under given circumstances. Character is formed and reformed over a lifetime. Choice is a free act of the self as a whole with its acquired character. A decision is both a specific act of choice by the self as subject and at the same time an expression of a formed character structure. Decisions are free and determined, since freedom is nothing more or less than self-determination. Decisions have as much predictability and

formed character structure

consistency as our character structure possesses over time. We cannot alter this pattern of priorities in any given moment by just deciding to do so. What we do expresses what we are, and we cannot fundamentally alter what we are in a moment by merely deciding to do so. We cannot choose to hate what we love or love what we hate by just doing it.

Self-rule functions, then, within the limits defined by the prioritized organization of aims, norms, inhibitions, and motivations that comprise a given person. Although the center constituted by the dominant features of character tends to remain more or less steady under normal circumstances, the range of permissible and mandated alternatives may be fluid or vague or shifting, especially at the outer margins. This latter fact may give rise to the feeling that some choices are purely arbitrary. They seem to the decision-maker at that moment totally uncaused, unaffected by anything other than the sheer act of selection exercised by an autonomous free will. A deeper analysis might reveal a situation of energetic fluctuation in the strength of particular guiding tendencies rather than the mere absence of any governing structure. Any specific choice both constitutes and registers the dominant activating motive at that moment in a dynamically organized structure that is here being called character. A unity between the governed and the governing self is created at the moment of decision that may or may not be identical with another outcome under approximately the same conditions earlier or later.

Every self, then, has an operational *Gestalt,* an ensemble of predispositions, passions, proclivities, and preferences that may or may not be subservient to some sovereign aim or norm. These master purposes, ideals, and standards that constitute character regulate human choice and action. These overarching directing aims may exhibit varying degrees of inconsistency, conflict, complexity, ambiguity, and ambivalence in the decision-making process. These guiding tendencies are dynamically arranged, and their strength in relation to competing propensities may shift. We may not be aware of or fully understand what actually motivates us to act as we do in some cases. The field of forces that constitutes character functions at both conscious and unconscious levels. The formative energies that constitute preference and guide decision intrude into awareness in varying degrees. Cognizance may range from the clarity of precise self-conscious commitments to the vagueness of a barely felt urge from the dimmer areas of comprehension beyond articulation that recedes finally into utter unconsciousness.

Free choices are simply the total self expressing itself in actions living out its own distinctive character with its distinctive set of aims, motives, beliefs, principles, and norms. The self in choosing is governed by character, while choice activates, confirms, and validates character. Choice is not coerced automatically or mechanically by character but rather is ratified and sometimes reformed by the self-transcending self in acts of free decision. The deciding self stands above its character with its dominant motives at the same time that it is guided by them. Character, however, is complex and may be made up of elements neither fully organized nor harmonized with the whole. Hence, the presence of inner dissension or chaos may produce erratic behavior confusing to observers as well as to the self. Unconscious motives in conflict with rational desire may produce neurotic complications. Unfortunately, formed character may also contain a demonic element that operates to produce tragic results.

Decision-making involves the creation and selection of the best means to achieve given ends. Or it may involve intentional thought to discover the most fitting expression of our norms, obligations, and commitments. Such choice may involve rational calculation designed to ascertain the best way to get what we desire, do our duty, and so on. Considerable creativity may be displayed in the process of finding the most appropriate and effective manifestation of the self's aims, norms, and commitments.

Choice, then, is directed by character. What we are governs what we do. I take this to be what Jesus meant when he said that a good tree brings forth good fruit. Hence, freedom is not a matter of making up our minds in a finite type of *creatio ex nihilo* in each particular situation as it arises. Rather we should think in terms of patterns of behavior that express character structure contextually.

A pedophile guilty of numerous offenses does not just randomly or by chance decide over and over again to molest a child. This kind of repetitive act does not just happen by accident or arbitrarily. While a choice is made in each instance, this persistent habit exhibits a deep-rooted element in a perverted personality formation. This is why we need to speak of the demonic as a factor that enters into decision-making in such cases. A kind person does not capriciously decide by happenstance on each occasion to be compassionate and gentle, as if being cruel were a real option, but creatively lives out an acquired virtue in ways appropriate to each new circumstance.

Our choices have a general but not absolute or static order and predictability about them, so that if we know people well enough we can have a pretty good idea about how they will react to particular situations. It is this *Gestalt* quality about decision-making that gives consistency to our attitudes and actions. These patterns of choice are distinctive to each individual. At the same time the more people share the same immediate or local culture and the same social status (race, nationality, sex, class, education, etc.), the more they are likely to think and act alike. Perhaps we all have a common nature marked by a set of deep underlying tendencies and predispositions that identify us as human beings, however much we may be molded by our cultural inheritance and individual life histories.

Character structure from person to person will show immense variation in detail. Any particular *Gestalt* may be highly complex, with multiple conflicts, competing elements, ambivalences, and confusions. Most of us have mixed feelings about a lot of things that complicate our decision-making. We should think of loose congeries of tendencies, preferences, and motivations dynamically organized around various levels of directing norms and guiding goals. Character is not a hard and fast, rigidly ordered system of priorities grouped in strict hierarchical fashion. Along with dominant inclinations may be latent proclivities, so that given different provocations, one or the other may be elicited and reflected in choice and action. Not to be omitted are those obsessions and compulsions that make us act repeatedly against our better

50

judgment in obedience to these irresistible urges. In short, character structure may comprise varying degrees and types of harmony and conflict.

We may act erratically, impulsively, and capriciously. Hence, an unpredictable element always attends freedom. It feels like a certain amount of looseness or "play," defined as "freedom of movement within a limited space," attends our ability to choose.[7] This is related to the fact that the self as acting subject always stands above the self as observed object with its character and motives. The nuances, variations, and subtleties surrounding this aspect of freedom are beyond simple summary or description. Nevertheless, what feels like mere whim or arbitrary selection is not likely to violate the overarching set of governing ends, obligations, preferences, and passions that guides normal choice.

2. Creative Choice. Freedom also involves the capacity to create a new *Gestalt,* to reorient the self around a new ensemble of motives, values, aims, and norms. Reorganizations of character structure occur at varying levels of importance and comprehensiveness. Radical conversions are rare. More frequent are the minor modifications in beliefs, values, and attitudes that most people go through over a lifetime. Character changes may occur when, for whatever reasons, the previously effective system becomes unsatisfactory, unworkable, or too full of anomalies to serve the larger and deeper ends, needs, and wants of the self. A creative transcendence of the dissatisfied self may take place by an imaginative construction of a fresh *Gestalt* around a novel organizing center of aims, preferences, and commitments. This reconstitution of character may be experienced as a spontaneous conversion. This is the operation of the self-transcending self at its highest and marks the distinguishing feature of human beings in relation to what we know or suspect about other animals. Simpler self-transforming activities similar in some respects, however, may occur at many levels of nature.[8] New forms of organization have emerged, for example, in the evolutionary process.

In human beings a self-conscious, deliberately self-directed process is involved in creative self-transformation that presumably is not present in analogous occurrences in the non-human world.

The creation of a new *Gestalt*, however, is not arbitrary or uncaused even in this case but emerges out of the quest for the perceived highest good relevant to the situation. It has the character, however, of a new creation.

It is worth emphasizing that the self cannot by merely taking thought change the actually functioning *Gestalt*. The most drastic transformations occur when the operational system of motives, aims, impulses, and commitments breaks down in the presence of promising alternatives, prompting a creative reorganization of character by an imaginative leap of the will. Other changes may transpire when more attractive possibilities arise through experience and changing circumstances. Everyone who has been liberated from some unwanted or neurotic pattern of behavior knows that change is not easy. We do not always understand just how it comes about. Often it feels more like a gift than an achievement, although deliberate effort and consciously employed techniques can help in some cases.

In summary, we are gifted with a capacity of creative self-transcendence that enables us to alter the self-guided trajectory of our lives. Conversion and new birth do occur. Change, however, presupposes a set of facilitating conditions that we cannot by merely wishing bring into existence. Transformations may occur gradually as dissatisfaction or new insight leads to the adoption of different norms, goals, or means. More dramatic instances of change occur when the currently functioning configuration breaks down and is restructured as newly attractive possibilities are imaginatively entertained and existentially enacted.[9] These changes, whether great or small, may be beneficial or detrimental to self or society. Tragically, some may be so enslaved by destructive patterns rooted in their past that positive change may be difficult, even impossible. This is the remnant of experiential truth in the old doctrine of predestination by which some are damned.

We are responsible for what we do in the sense that what we choose expresses what we are. This does not mean that in every circumstance we could have done differently from what we did in actual practice, though in principle and abstractly other possibilities were open to us. In other cases, we clearly could have chosen differently. Character guides but does not coercively dictate. The creative, autonomous, self-transcending self does the choosing. In any case, since we are self-determining in our actions, we are accountable for them. A fine line may separate our being unable to choose better than we do and our being unwilling to do so.

RESPONSIBILITY AND GUILT

To return to the story with which this chapter began, the teenager who unmercifully killed the old woman made a choice in that situation to do what she did. Yet her act was an expression of a character formation that permitted murder. Her life up to that point had created in her a potential for cruelty. Murder was a possibility not ruled out by moral constraints effectively operating within her. Most people could not bring themselves to do what she did, including many who may have had an equally traumatic or destructive family history. They could not arbitrarily choose to go out and kill someone. Their character with its system of moral guidance would not allow it. Her life history, including her own previous choices, had obviously created this option, else she could not have done it. What were the ingredients in this horrible configuration that created the potential for this dreadful deed — hurt that had created latent hostile energies, a sense of power-lessness to resist the devastating forces that had shattered her childhood, shame, loss of self-esteem, a destructive past that had led to feelings of the absurdity, meaningless, and purposeless of her existence and a nihilistic, don't care, nothing matters anyway, life is hell attitude with associated feelings of blind destructiveness and inner rage? What it was that overwhelmed her moral sensibilities so that she could not feel concern for the woman she viciously attacked we can only guess. I don't know what went on within her, but something terrible in her experience had led to a character formation with this potential. My assumption is that elements of the tragic and the demonic, as these terms are to be defined later on, were present in her life and in this awful deed.

Could she have done otherwise? Could she have restrained herself and refused to express her inner pain and rage in this fashion in this immediate situation? I want to say that she could have chosen otherwise than she did. Did some irresistible compulsion strike her at the moment that rendered her incapable of rational thought and moral judgment? Perhaps, I don't know. Even if we knew her life story in detail and had the most skilled psychiatrist probe her conscious and unconscious mind to discern the inner psychic forces, feelings, thoughts, and mental processes that had created her personality and character, we perhaps could not render a certain judgment as to whether she had the power of contrary choice in that old woman's kitchen. A line between unwilling and unable does exist. Which sides of the line she was on, we cannot say with certainty.

We can say that she was responsible for what she did, since her act expressed her being. What we do manifests who and what we are. It was her choice to murder, and even if she could not have done otherwise, it was she who decided and acted. She — the same person in the courtroom as the person who murdered — cannot be separated from her deed. Holding her accountable does not settle the terribly difficult problem of how she should be treated by society.

I think we need to develop a notion of "tragic sin." Disastrous life circumstances may so overwhelm some persons that their capacity for doing good and avoiding evil in some cases is effectively negated. Their sin is tragic because it is unavoidable. They must be held responsible but not guilty.[10] They are responsible not only because they factually did the deeds but also because these acts express what they really are or have become.[11] They are not guilty (blameworthy) if calamitous life circumstances have so overwhelmed them that their capacity to act morally in some circumstances is effectively negated. The diminishment of moral capacity under the circumstances given their total genetic makeup and life history flowed from causes over which they had no control. They are the author of wrongdoing but not culpable, i.e., not condemnable. Such persons are more to be pitied than censored. To the degree that this occurs in any person, both the tragic and the demonic are exemplified. Whether this young woman's horrible deed was an instance of tragic sin, I cannot say.

Immense practical problems arise here related both to our inability to know precisely when the line between unwilling and unable is crossed in specific cases and our perplexity in knowing how to deal with people practically in the home, in the courts, at work, and on the streets in the presence of tragic and demonic sin. In normal practice, I think we have to proceed as if people are equally gifted in moral capacity and treat everyone by the same standards of accountability until we have compelling reason to believe otherwise. In the courts we have to assume that persons who commit crimes could have chosen to do otherwise, except in exceptional circumstances in which the evidence for diminished moral and mental capacity is overwhelming.[12] The exact truth will often be beyond our ability to discern. People may differ in moral capacity as much as in physical ability and mental prowess. Our moral proficiency may vary widely, based on genetic inheritance, cultural heritage, family training, life experience, past choice and effort, and so on. Why should we think that our moral competence would not show as much variety as our aptitude for hitting a baseball or solving complex mathematical puzzles?

Since we lack exact and verifiable knowledge of the moral aptitude of persons precisely nuanced to fit each individual, we have to start with guidelines applicable to everyone and modify them cautiously and only when evidence compels us to do so. Nevertheless, what we do know about some things does have practical implications. To take one example, the fact that instances of murder are far more prevalent in some zip codes than in others is not accidental. The correlation of violent crime with family breakdown, social chaos, and economic distress should alert us to the fact that environmental factors influence behavior patterns. For the sensitive citizen this association of high rates of violence with certain statistical indices will suggest the need for wise social policy designed to improve the situation. Many of the arsonists responsible for burning African-American churches in the South present a troubling profile — white, young, poor, little education, unemployed or working for low wages, and with no previous criminal record but angry or drinking heavily at the time.[13] The connection of destructive and undesirable conduct with harsh, frustrating living conditions will continue to challenge the moral philosopher in search of the meaning, the scope, and the limits of human freedom and responsibility.

From this discussion of the nature of human freedom and the meaning of responsibility, we now turn to the use made of freedom in relation to sin, injustice, and the demonic.

---

1. The examples that follow were taken from the *Democrat and Chronicle* of Rochester, New York (May 29, 1994), 13A.

2. Here I follow Reinhold Niebuhr, *The Nature and Destiny of Man* (New York: Charles Scribner's Sons, 1949), I:1-77. The further use of the concept is my responsibility alone and is not intended to be mere exegesis of Niebuhr.

3. Paul Tillich, *Systematic Theology* (Chicago: University of Chicago Press, 1951), I:182-186.

4. *Ibid.*, 185.

5. I am inclined to believe that Alfred North Whitehead is correct in affirming that freedom in this general sense is present at every level of nature right down through the molecular and atomic levels, i.e., as far as is necessary to reach the simplest "actual entity." See his *Process and Reality* (New York: The Macmillan Co., 1929). Freedom is also a universal category in the ontology of Paul Tillich. See *Systematic Theology,* I:182-186. Whitehead is a panpsychist, while for Tillich mentality is an emergent. Each view has conceptual advantages the other lacks, with no possibility for resolving the issue for sure.

6. Determinism associated with reductionism is current among many scientists. The mechanists among them are persuaded that the decisive explanations of everything human are ultimately in terms of the laws of physics and chemistry. According to some, then, the organism as a whole is the servant of the systems, organs, cells, molecules, atoms, and sub-atomic particles that compose the body. It is equally plausible to understand the parts of the body as servants of the organism as a whole, ideally functioning in harmony to sustain and promote the interests of the body-self as a total system. It certainly appears that when I try to hit a baseball with a bat that I am making a purposive decision that guides the actions of the eyes, the arms, the muscles, and so on

that carry out the effort. Both perspectives are surely needed in a complete explanatory scheme. For a more detailed discussion and for a defense of what I call strong organicism, see my *Theological Biology*, 191-220.

7. See meanings 16, 17, and 18 in *The American College Dictionary* (New York: Random House, 1949), 929.

8. See, for example, Arthur Peacocke, *God and the New Biology* (San Francisco: Harper & Row, 1986), 133-160.

9. The process I refer to here is analogous to what Thomas Kuhn calls a "paradigm shift." See his *The Structure of Scientific Revolutions*. 2nd ed. (Chicago: University of Chicago Press, 1970).

10. Responsible has a variety of meanings, including the following: (1) factually the cause or author of something, (2) answerable for something under one's power or control, and (3) not only capable but trustworthy. Guilty has at least two meanings: (1) factually having done something wrong or criminal and (2) deserving of censure or condemnation. In order to make myself clear, I have to make use of some of these definitions and avoid others. At this particular point, I am using responsibility in sense (1) and guilty in sense (2) above.

11. The notion that we should hate the sin but love the sinner is a useful practical maxim, but it involves an abstraction that too neatly and wrongly separates the act from the agent.

12. The courts, guided by laws that have developed over the centuries, have their own ways of dealing with responsibility and guilt. I do not here enter that thorny and complicated area.

13. *USA Today* (July 1, 1996), 1A-2A. Prof. Jack Levin of Northeastern University, who has studied hate crimes, claims that 65% spring from teenage boredom, often fueled by anger and drinking. The phenomenon of church burnings, however, is complex. No simple or singular explanation fits them all. Some are racially motivated; most are not. Some black churches have been torched by black people. Insurance company officials, while noting an increase in 1995-1996, observe that the number of church fires is within expected ranges over recent years. Houses of worship of every faith and race have been burned. Churches are easy targets and have always been a favorite of arsonists and thrill seekers who love fire but do not discriminate on racial or religious grounds. *Democrat and Chronicle,* Rochester, New York (July 7, 1996), 11A, 15A.

Chapter Four

The Meaning Of Sin: The Mystery Of Iniquity

Shortly after 9:00 a.m. on April 19, 1995, a Ryder rental truck filled with perhaps 4,800 pounds of explosives became an awful detonating bomb that ripped away half of the nine-story Murrah Federal Building in Oklahoma City. The death toll mounted and eventually rose to 168. Many of the dead were children who had just been left in a day care center by trusting parents. Men and women in masks sifted through the wreckage looking for clues that might help solve the crime. They stumbled upon pieces of dead bodies amid stench and decay with dimming hopes that survivors might still be found in the rubble. The whole nation was in mourning over the devastation, destruction, and immense suffering the citizens of that city and state underwent. It was a deliberate act requiring planning and skill. It was committed by human beings whose aim was to kill and destroy for reasons not yet fully known and that will never be fully understood by the grieving victims who were innocent of any wrongdoing against the perpetrators. President Clinton told the nation that the bombing was evil.

CHRISTIAN PERSPECTIVES ON SIN

Freedom implies the capacity to do good and to do evil. In theological terms, the evil that springs from freedom is called **sin**, and its social expression is **injustice**. Its tragic manifestation is the **demonic**. Generally speaking, sin refers to any failure of human beings to live as God intended. It is a disruption of the normative relationship between the self, God, and other people. In its broadest meaning, it also includes alienation from nature and other life. Sin, then, is an all-encompassing state of estrangement involving all connections and interactions that define what human life ought to be. More narrowly, it is a failure of people to love God with their whole being and their neighbors as themselves. Within this framework, sin has a religious dimension and a moral dimension. Religiously, sin involves a choice that distorts the relation of the self to God. Unbelief or distrust, idolatry, pride, rebellion, and disobedience are typical ways this perversion is expressed. Morally, sin is a choice that distorts the ideal relation of the self to other people and does harm to them. It is a self-centered orientation that neglects, ignores, or subverts the rights, needs, distress, and want of others so that one's own selfish ambitions can be realized. If all forms of its expression have a common feature, it is an orientation that makes the self and the communities with which the self identifies the center of value. This disordering produces a systemic distortion of the dispositions, attitudes, motivations, choices, and actions of people in relationship to God and each other. While not everyone would employ the same categories and forms of expression, wide agreement among Christians would be found at this level of generality.

Beyond this, extensive differences of opinion come into view. The major points of controversy can be highlighted by examining three traditions that have been prominent over the centuries: the Pelagian, the Augustinian, and the Irenaean. The first two get their names from the early fifth century dispute between Pelagius, a British monk, and Augustine, the Bishop of Hippo. The third is based on the outlook of Irenaeus, the Bishop of Lyons, who lived in the latter part of the second century.[1] I shall focus not on their particular views but on the type of approach each represents. It is the model itself and its dominant assumptions that are important. Representatives of each of these orientations can be found across time from the early centuries until the present.

1. THE PELAGIANS

The Pelagians have the simplest view: sin is the deliberate violation of a known law that we could have obeyed. If wrongdoing proceeds from necessity, it is not sin. If it proceeds from freedom, it is avoidable. Pelagians believe that the will is weak though disposed toward goodness or at least not corrupt at birth. Nevertheless, it can be easily dragged down or seduced by nature or by the social environment. Unless we can avoid doing wrong, however, God does not hold us responsible and does not consider us sinful. Pelagius and his followers believed that the sin of Adam and Eve affected them only, except as their defection constituted a bad example leading to corrupt social practices that adversely influenced subsequent generations. Put more abstractly, for the Pelagian outlook sin is the victory of nature over spirit. Biological impulses, natural inertia, personal frailty, and the sheer difficulty of living virtuously tempt a weak will to give consent to wrong-doing. Modern Pelagians under the influence of evolutionary theory reason that human nature is not corrupt but atavistic, i.e., strongly influenced toward base behavior by the beastly impulses of our pre-human ancestors.[2]

2. THE AUGUSTINIANS

The Augustinians believe we all inevitably sin by choice. It is at least experientially paradoxical, if not an offense to logic, to affirm both unavoidable universality and individual responsibility. Augustine said that after Adam and Eve people are free only to sin, since all have inherited a corrupt nature from the first parents. Yet God holds us responsible and deems us worthy of condemnation. John Calvin pushes the logical difficulties of the Augustinian view to the furthest extreme possible. All since Adam and Eve are born with a corrupt nature, therefore sin inevitably proceeds from this inherited depravity (original sin). Nevertheless, since we transgress voluntarily, we are held strictly accountable for our actions. At a deeper level, however, God decrees whatever comes to pass, including the fall in Eden and our own trespasses.

In the Augustinian view the will is strong but corrupt. The crucial point is that the will is corrupted by its own act so that the whole system of decision-making is distorted. Sin is serious since it proceeds from a defect at the center of personality. The locus of sin is in the will itself. Sin is the turning of the will away from God toward the self. All choices and acts that proceed from this systemic perversion are tainted with rebelliousness toward God and disregard for the moral law. The essence of sin is unbelief (distrust of God) and pride (inordinate love of self) that produces a totally disordered soul and issues forth in insatiable sensuality and all forms of unlawfulness and immorality. In making sin unavoidable, Augustinians imply a tragic dimension to human existence. Many followed Augustine in arguing that "God judged it better to bring good out of evil than to suffer no evil to exist." Hence, sin is instrumental to a larger good.

Modern theologians consider the Genesis story of Adam and Eve to be a myth, i.e., not literally true but filled with truth about our present existence. Neo-Augustinians, of whom Reinhold Niebuhr is the most brilliant representative, do not believe that we inherit a corrupt nature from our parents. Nevertheless, existing at the junction of freedom and necessity, spirit and nature, we are made anxious by self-awareness of our situation. We can envision possibilities of good that we cannot with certainty attain. We can anticipate possibilities of disaster and destruction, including death itself, that we cannot with certainty avoid. The anxiety that accompanies our existence in finite freedom becomes the internal precondition of sin and the occasion of temptation. Rebellion and disobedience are the inevitable outcome. The ideal possibility of resolving our anxiety in trust in divine love is universally bypassed. Instead, unbelief, pride, injustice, and sensuality define the response of all. Yet we could have done otherwise.

Since we are powerfully tempted, sin is not sheer perversity. Yet, despite temptation, nothing causes us to sin. It is not necessary for us to respond in this fashion. In the situation of anxiety and temptation, sin posits itself (Kierkegaard); it just jumps into the situation. According to Niebuhr, sin, then, is inevitable but not necessary. It is a spiritual certainty but is not determined by internal or external forces nor caused by overpowering physical or spiritual compulsion. Sin proceeds from choice, but inevitably and universally we elect to rebel against God and disobey. He holds that we are responsible despite this unavoidability. The proof of responsibility despite inevitability is the identification we make with our sinful acts after the fact in the feeling of remorse for our wrongdoing.[3]

3. THE IRENAEANS

The Irenaeans believe that Adam and Eve, whether the Genesis story is taken literally or symbolically, were not mature adults but like children. Their failure is not surprising. Because, like them, we enter the world immature, ignorant, and inexperienced, it is understandable and virtually inevitable that we will sin in our efforts to grow toward maturity. Moreover, God planned it that way. The divine aim is to perfect us as moral personalities who by our own free choice come to love God and each other. Sin and suffering are essential to the process of soul-making by which we are purified and perfected. Evil is a necessary teaching aid that helps us eventually find our way to God. The world, then, is a laboratory of soul-making. Sin and suffering are permitted if not ordained by God as a part of the design by which we are to be eventually led to faith and loving relationships with God and neighbor.

Modern Irenaeans find the evolutionary view of human origins congenial to their outlook. The human race emerged gradually from its animal background and had to find its way in the midst of ignorance, uncertainty, and difficulty. Initially, we exist in a state of "epistemic distance" from God, since the world gives at best ambiguous evidence of divine goodness. We have no certainty that God is loving and trustworthy. The hope is that in the end all will finally choose the life of love in the presence of alternatives and despite uncertainty about the ultimate facts. Only universal redemption will satisfy this scheme, since anything less would be a failure of divine purpose. In the end when all human beings have at long last achieved moral perfection in a heavenly world, the sin, massive miseries, and absurd evils of earthly life will in retrospective glance fade into insignificance. In short, the facts of life are such that the only road to heaven goes right through a valley almost certainly filled with sin, suffering, and evil.[4]

EVALUATION

All three of these perspectives contain insights that must be preserved in an adequate, comprehensive doctrine.

1. THE PELAGIANS

The Pelagians are right in rejecting the Augustinian notion of inherited depravity and guilt. Evolutionary theory dispels the notion of a literal Adam and Eve. Moreover, it is irrational and wrong to hold that people are blameworthy before God for what they cannot help doing as a consequence of a corrupt nature they were born with because of the defection of the primal parents. They are correct also in seeing that the embeddedness of the human spirit in a finite body with its natural impulses creates a downward inertial drag on moral aspiration. The human spirit is weak and vulnerable to adverse environmental influences and degrading life histories associated with poverty, violence, destructive family life, and social chaos. The correlation of crime rates with degrading social conditions cannot be ignored. When Pelagian recognition of human weakness and vulnerability is combined with the Irenaean insight that the human race, as well as each new individual, begins life inexperienced, ignorant, naive, and with undeveloped faculties of mind and conscience, we have an ingredient essential for a proper starting point. We begin life as a race and as an individual innocent, naive, ignorant, and inexperienced. Given the difficulties and challenges of becoming a mature moral person, wholesome and loving, it is no wonder that we develop warped values and fall into error, prejudice, and iniquity.

To their credit, Pelagians and Irenaeans are more sympathetic to human frailty. Asserting that sin springing from freedom not finitude is the basic problem, Augustinians show no mercy, holding an unrealistically high view of freedom and human capacities in the face of existential terrors and extenuating circumstances. Niebuhr admits the terrors but thinks that, ideally, we could choose faith and justice despite the profound anxieties that accompany human existence.

Nevertheless, the Pelagian outlook tends toward a superficial rationalism and moralism, even legalism, that ignores the deeper mysteries of iniquity and its tragic dimension. The question of human responsibility given the life circumstances over which we have no control that condition and shape behavior is baffling. Pelagians hold people responsible only for deliberate and avoidable violations of a known law. Modern Augustinians like Reinhold Niebuhr teach responsibility despite inevitability, since the unavoidability of sin is rooted in freedom and not in nature or circumstance. Both outlooks have the virtue of preserving the link between responsibility and freedom, since in either case we could have done otherwise. However, in Niebuhr's view sin is, paradoxically, tragic (inevitable) and not tragic (freely chosen). In the previous chapter I have argued on a doggedly empirical and Pelagian basis for a notion of "tragic sin" for which we must be held responsible but not blameworthy.

Finally, the Pelagian viewpoint in its purest forms leans toward an atomistic or nominalistic approach in which each moral choice is a separate, discrete point of decision. This obscures the systemic corruption, i.e., the defects of character structure, from which particular acts of wrongdoing spring. It was this recognition that led Paul Tillich, a neo-Augustinian, to suggest that we should never speak of sins in the plural but always of Sin as a total state of estranged existence. Tillich's point is valid, yet it offends the Pelagian and common sense empirical observation that people sometimes do good deeds and at other times commit wrong acts. Both insights have to be preserved.

2. THE AUGUSTINIANS

The Augustinians are accurate in locating the origin of sin in the depths of the human spirit self-corrupted by false choices. This is their foremost insight. This is the standard paradigm, the working norm that we must assume in healthy people. The Pelagians are right in seeing the will as weak and vulnerable. Nevertheless, it is capable of creative perversity in the pursuit of selfish ends, although it may be enslaved by demonic powers or overwhelmed by tragic circumstances. The consequence of sinful choice is a systematic distortion that creates a pattern of destructive and disordered living that affects every area of existence. Finally, modern existentialist

Augustinians helpfully point to anxiety as constituting temptation to sin in a futile attempt to achieve security and tranquility in the midst of the terrors of existence.

By recognizing the depth, persistence, and seriousness of sin, Augustinians are able to account for the massive evils of history more adequately than a shallow Pelagianism ever could. However, in teaching a strict doctrine of the inevitability and universality of sin, an unnecessary offense to logic is created. Reinhold Niebuhr protests that logic has no resources to express the experiential truth that sin is inevitable but not necessary. This is not ultimately satisfactory. It is better to render Niebuhr's logical incongruity harmless by saying that sin is an overwhelming probability and therefore likely to be universal. This Pelagian maneuver preserves free choice and makes universality an empirical matter.

Paul Tillich proposes that sinful choice is both a free decision and a tragic fact universal in scope.[5] This means that "actualized creation and estranged existence are identical." He thus becomes vulnerable to Niebuhr's charge that sin becomes an ontological necessity. Tillich's response is that the transition from created goodness to fallen existence is a leap made in freedom and not a "structural necessity." Yet when he speaks of the "coincidence of creation and the Fall" and writes that all actualized existence is estranged, it certainly sounds, despite his protests, like "sin is an ontological necessity rather than a matter of personal responsibility." He claims that the factual coincidence of creation and fall is not a logical coincidence but has the character of a leap of freedom. Whether this is more than a verbal dodge is not apparent to me. In the end, like Niebuhr, he takes the risk of falling into rational absurdity for the sake of preserving existential truth. Tillich affirms that creation is essentially good, but this unblemished goodness is non-historical and non-empirical in terms of fact. More precisely, it is empirical and historical in terms of potential only, since all actualized existence is estranged.

Put otherwise, all real life, all actualized fact, is at best ambiguous. Tillich knows all this as a matter of metaphysical truth and certainty, not as an empirical conclusion based on observation, and that is my problem with him. Tillich admits that analysis in terms of essence and existence is abstract. Actual concrete life unites essence and existence in dynamic and complex ways but always in estrangement, so that everything real is at most ambiguously good. Apparently, Tillich holds that there is a pattern for the absolutely ideal apple, an essence of what an apple truly and deeply is and ought to be. However, nowhere has there ever been, nor could there be, a concretely real existing apple that measures up fully to this absolute ideal. All have some flaw; all are estranged from this essence. All apples in real life are only ambiguously good.

I no longer find this Platonic language useful. This scheme enables Tillich to know in advance as a matter of universal principle that "life" — the realm of concretely actual beings —is never quite what it ought to be and really is essentially. Ambiguity is an important category for me and is pervasive in life. Nevertheless, I prefer a stubborn and persistent empiricism that seeks to determine in particular cases where ambiguity is present and in what manner and to what degree. This approach is more tentative and eschews generalizations that have the character of absoluteness. Tillich denies that he deduces universal ambiguity from the principles of a systematic ontology that dictates conclusions that follow by necessity. Nevertheless, while he insists that it occurs through freedom in unity with destiny, he knows with predictable certainty that all existence is estranged existence, that all life is ambiguous.[6] How can he be so sure? I do not find it useful to think of apples or cats or musical compositions or anything else, including human beings and their goodness or sinfulness, in this logically precise fashion.[7]

Neither Niebuhr nor Tillich can escape the Pelagian indictment of neo-liberals that making sin inevitable or tragically unavoidable compromises the goodness of creation. To avoid this consequence as well as logical contradiction, it is better to approach universality in terms of empirical probability. Whether one speaks of sin as a spiritual inevitability flowing from freedom (Niebuhr) or as a tragically universal transition from essence to existence that characterizes the actualization of creation (Tillich), the consequence is that sin can be predicted of all people in advance as a matter of strict certainty. Whether presented in terms of a metaphysical system reflecting a Platonic ancestry (Tillich) or put in more dramatic, historical terminology as a postulate about human spirit (Niebuhr), the result is the same. Any future event that can be predicted with absolute and guaranteed certainty as a matter of principle cannot by ordinary means of reckoning also be the consequence of free choice, even a Tillichian "leap." What would Niebuhr have lost if he had said that, given the juxtaposition of natural finitude and spiritual freedom that defines human existence, sin is well-nigh inevitable and almost certain?

3. THE IRENAEANS

The Irenaean perspective aptly describes the evolutionary origins of humanity and correctly reflects the fact that each individual begins life as an infant. Human personality is a historical emergent. Hence, it is appropriate to see the human race as a whole and each self as coming to moral consciousness naive, ignorant, inexperienced, gullible, immature, and prone to error and sin. Tillich's notion that Adam and Eve before the fall lived in a state of "dreaming innocence" whose human potentials are as yet unactualized has an Irenaean flavor. "Dreaming innocence" also characterizes each new child who has not yet made significant life decisions. Tillich uses the instance of a young person prior to having sexual knowledge and experience as an example. Once decisions are made experientially, innocence is lost and ambiguity emerges. (I would say in all probability emerges to some extent.) This is a proper starting point for thinking about sin. However, the further claims of a modern Irenaean like John Hick that sin and suffering are not only inevitable but part of a divine plan to perfect us as moral personalities through a process of choice, growth, and maturation must be firmly rejected. It is preferable to say that God chose to create despite the risk that sin, evil, and suffering are so highly probable as to be nearly certain.

Moreover, the Augustinian category of "the fall" should be abandoned for Irenaean reasons. A state of perfection never existed historically and is not useful even as a symbolic or mythical category. Humanity did not fall from some primordial state of natural goodness, nor does each new individual person born into the world. The human situation is not that we tumble from some perfected state of actuality but that we do not rise up to actualize our fullest potential for goodness, morality, justice, and happiness. Sin is a failure of freedom to actualize the ideal possibilities that emerge in the process of living. Individuals choose less than the best possible for themselves and others in a given situation or over a lifetime. Societies fail to achieve the potential given with their resources for justice, well-being, and the fullest flowering of human capabilities for truth, goodness, and beauty over generations.

FURTHER REFLECTIONS

More must be said. Sin is not merely a failure to achieve the best that is morally and spiritually possible. That alone is too negative. The creative imagination can hardly escape being fascinated by the possibilities of exploiting the potential for selfish gain and glory even at the expense of others. It is simply the case that one's own good is intrinsically more attractive as a motivating goal than the good of our neighbors. This is especially the case with neighbors at a distance whom we do not love as much as we love ourselves. That includes nearly everyone outside the immediate family and/or maybe rarely some very close friends. Hardly ever do we love the children of other people with the same fervor as we love our own.

Moral evil is also creative perversity, intentional injury, and deliberate cruelty. Sin includes fanatical craving for power, glory, eminence, honor, and every form of self-aggrandizement. It refers to oppression, injustice, domination, and tyranny motivated by voracious selfishness, and insatiable greed. It is rapacious sensuality and the unquenchable quest for luxury, comfort, and pleasure often sought at the expense and neglect of others. We have to account for the abuse and murder of children by parents, for the rape, slaughter, and mutilation of women by serial killers, for ethnic and racial hatred, genocidal wars, bloody territorial conflicts, for all the violent, destructive behavior, and for every other form of moral depravity to which history gives ample and sickening evidence. This makes the Augustinian account of human iniquity profoundly and perennially relevant, despite its limitations.

Yet moral evil is not always sheer perversity. The existentialists are right. Anxious insecurity is the experiential concomitant of finite freedom become self-aware. This gives vehemence and energy to the tempting quest for tranquility born of power and the possession of money, goods, and territory by which want, danger, and other people cease to be threats to our serenity. Moreover, the likelihood that patterns of behavior destructive of self and others will develop may be increased by growing up in emotionally unhealthy families or pernicious social circumstances or cultures with perverted values. The presence of the demonic in selves and communities adds a tragic and, in this sense, unavoidable dimension to the evils found in life and history. Much sin proceeds from moral blindness and from enslavement to destructive patterns of behavior in individuals and groups as a consequence of demonic possession. Moral ambiguity adds a further tragic dimension of choice in so far as some positive gains cannot be had without loss or compromise of others. Ambiguous choices are found in every area of life at all levels of individual and communal existence, from individual life-choices to the complicated interactions of nation-states.

The Augustinian tradition has defined sin chiefly in terms of pride and unbelief. Pride is inordinate self-love. Self-exaltation expresses itself in a quest for excessive power used to dominate and exploit others. It takes the secondary form of sensuality — the selfish pursuit of pleasure, luxury, comfort, trivial diversion, or total immersion in worldly pursuits that devours life to the detriment of the human spirit and more lofty ambitions. Unbelief as lack of trust in and loyalty to God is the other side of pride as life centered on self and its egotistic purposes. Pride is turning away from God to the self and the groups with which it identifies as the locus of value.

Recently this outlook has come under criticism by feminist theologians. Their claim is that pride and the quest for dominating power are the peculiar sins of men and do not necessarily apply equally to women. The sin of females is more likely to be self-abnegation or neglect of self rather than self-elevation. Passivity, timidity, triviality, submissive consent to a subservient status, collaboration with male oppressors for secondary gains or to avoid humiliation or conflict are the typical ways that the failure of women to claim their self-worth and dignity may be expressed.[8] Valid points are being made here. The crucial one is that sin may take two forms: self-exaltation and self-abdication. Both are distorted expressions of a just and balanced concern for self in relation to others. Failure to claim and develop one's freedom and potential is just as improper as extravagant self-love that seeks power in order to dominate and exploit other people.

Whether the prideful exercise of force in contrast to passivity and self-denial are characteristics of men and women respectively as genetic traits is quite another question. It is likely but not certain that these different forms of self-distortion reflect social facts more than sexual distinctiveness, although both may be involved. We should not rule out a genetic or biological factor as a factor in creating predispositions to act in certain typical ways. Men may, generally speaking, approach life differently from women, allowing for individual variations. I suspect that prideful self-exaltation may be the peculiar sin of those with power while timid self-negation may be more associated with individuals and groups without controlling strength. Or the contrast may reflect differences in individual temperament, life history, choice, social location, cultural background, and so on as well as or instead of innate sexual difference genetically inherited.

The recognition that sin may vary in its characteristic expression according to gender and social location opens up the wider question as to whether it is uniform in other respects as well. The usual assumption in scholarly and colloquial discussion is that an essence called human nature is present with identical features in all.[9] This "one size fits all" is probably not the appropriate paradigm. It may be that self-elevation is the chief sin of some and self-abnegation of others in ways sometimes related to sex or social status and sometimes not. Prideful self-assertion and sensual indulgence may be present in all to some degree, but the priority, frequency, and intensity of each probably varies widely. The main fault of some may be the aggressive domination of others for purposes of selfish gain. Others may be willing to live and let live, while quietly seeking comfort, pleasure, and luxury for themselves. Their sin is not so much the belligerent oppression but the passive neglect of others.

Anger, envy, gluttony, greed, lust, pride, and sloth are traditionally the deadly sins. However, the frequency and intensity with which these seven virulent transgressions are practiced may vary widely in the population. What is irresistible temptation for some may provoke indifference or disdain in others. Moreover, the capacity for moral achievement may well differ from one person to another based on nature, nurture, life history, and experience. Some may simply be more gifted from birth with the resources necessary to the development of moral insight and ethical skills in practice. The tendency toward sainthood may be inherited in some and a greater proclivity toward depravity in others. We have no standardized tests for measuring such things. Nevertheless, it should not be taken for granted that freedom, the capacity for loving God and neighbor, and sinful practice are the same in all human beings.

If a common feature exists in all forms of sin, it is probably inordinate self-concern. This means exaggerated preoccupation of individuals and groups with their own aims and interests in relation to the needs and just claims of others. This may involve aggressive pursuit of self-interest that uses power ruthlessly to dominate, control, and oppress others. Let us note, however, that self-abnegation, timidity, passivity, and trivial pursuits may also be a form of excessive focus on self. Failure to assert oneself or to confront oppressors may be a form of self-protection that serves self-interest in a negative, cowardly way. To accept passively one's assigned role in life, even if it is onerous, or to go along complacently in order to avoid trouble or conflict can also be an expression of undue self-concern. Life is easier that way, and that is a benefit, even if gained at a price.

In any case, whether truculently trespassing the boundaries of others to dominate and exploit or compliantly fitting in with the system and giving in to the needs or wishes of others, the common characteristic is an imbalance between self and others that promotes self-interest in unhealthy, destructive ways. Sometimes, however, a situation may be so oppressive that, in the face of overwhelming power, acceptance of one's lot may be a matter of sheer survival. In instances that offer no liberating alternative for the moment, acquiescence involves tragedy rather than guilt. Hence, while inordinate and unbalanced concern with self in relation to neighbor may be as close as we can come to a universal characterization of sin, we must be open to the intricate variety found in human experience. Otherwise, premature concern with theoretical simplicity may obscure the complexities and relativities of actual life.

So far this discussion runs the danger of being too abstract. We may get closer to the truth by becoming more deliberately empirical, historical, and developmental in approach. Individuals begin their lives in particular times, places, communities, and cultures. They grow up in families whose life-experiences and social circumstances subject them to an ensemble of values that may embody both constructive and destructive elements and that are in various combinations accepted, rejected, or modified. Patterns of behavior are formed that may display in various combinations both virtues and vices, habits of justice and of injustice, practices that honor and that show contempt for immediate neighbors and rival classes, races, nations, and religions. It is in some specific context that particular selves and communities acquire a character structure that may exhibit the sinful habits theologians describe in terms of *hubris* and estrangement (Paul Tillich), pride and sensuality (Reinhold Niebuhr), selfishness (Walter Rauschenbusch), self-abnegation (Judith Plaskow), oppression and injustice (liberation thinkers), and so on.

CONCLUSIONS

In summary, a combination of Pelagian, Augustinian, and Irenaean perspectives is most satisfactory. In particular three elements that enter into human perversity are worth noting. Here I speak of the norm, the standard paradigm of human existence and its predicament, not taking into account how particular life histories, social location, cultural conditioning, and the realities of race and gender may qualify the generalizations offered.

1. Human beings have an innate hunger for self-fulfillment, a deep inner *eros* that propels them toward the actualization of their potential for enjoyment. Biologically rooted, *eros* extends to every dimension of personhood. It reaches its noblest sublimated heights in the yearning of the spirit for the objectively true, the ultimately excellent, and the intrinsically beautiful. Nevertheless, since it is self-oriented in its basic tendency, the good of the self and of the communities to which the self belongs is intrinsically more attractive than the good of other selves and communities.

2. Natural *eros* is experienced in an atmosphere marked by existential apprehension. The self never fully escapes the anxiety generated by the consciousness of finitude and mortality, although this terror may reside at the fringes of awareness most of the time.[10] Anxiety may entice the self toward egocentric actions to protect and fortify the self and thus to reduce existential terror. Or anxiety may tempt the self to avoid danger by becoming harmless and seeking safe havens away from the storms and strife of life. This response is associated with a failure to confront evil and injustice — the sin of the timid and the passive. Neither *eros* nor anxiety are sin, but sin arises in the context of both. Their interwoven power constitutes a powerful temptation toward excessive self-regard.

3. In an atmosphere of anxiety, the natural *eros* that drives the self toward its own fulfillment is almost irresistibly magnified by human imagination and choice into inordinate self-concern that distorts the relation of the self to God and others. The transformation of the innate drive toward the good into excessive self-regard goes beyond what the healthy needs of the self require and usually results in injustice toward other people. Inordinate self-concern may take two forms.

(a) Natural self-centeredness may be transformed into the self-glorification Christian tradition has called spiritual pride, *hubris*. Selfishness and sensuality are its behavioral marks. Self-elevation prompts people to seek pleasure, money, power, material benefits, and psychic gains that tend toward a cherished superior-inferior relationship with others.[11] Collective aggression arising from *eros* compounded by *hubris* and mixed with anxiety issues forth in the illusive quest for an impregnable security and boundless glory to

74

produce history's great moral evils, as witnessed by the atrocities wrought by the modern nation-state in the twentieth century.

(b) The natural self-centeredness of *eros* may take the form of self-depreciation and exaggerated self-protectiveness. This timidity results in an avoidance of responsibility for the self or others or in a failure to actualize the self fully or in a fearful evasion of the duty to resist evil or in a collaboration with the powerful to secure secondary gains and to minimize threats to the self, or in similar derelictions.

In summary, evildoing is not the product of sheer perversity nor it is necessitated by human nature, although it may be deeply affected by the life histories of selves and communities. Rather, the natural bias of *eros* toward self in preference to the neighbor augmented by inordinate self-concern suffused with anxiety constitutes temptation that must be ratified by choice. Ideally, this narcissistic predisposition can be and often is overcome by love that creates an identity with the neighbor, by compassion that reaches out to relieve the suffering of others, and by an intuitive sense of the essential goodness and trustworthiness of life that nurtures tranquility of spirit. Love, compassion, and cosmic trust (faith in God) are likewise primordial human characteristics existing both as natural proclivities and as spiritual achievements. We do right and we do wrong by nature and by choice. Original evil, then, that produces harm to individuals, social injustice, and sometimes a trajectory of demonic power arises as a decision uniting freedom and destiny in selves in whom the fascinating enticement of self-love overwhelms equal or preferential regard for "the other."

FINAL REFLECTIONS

Can we ever fully understand what lies behind the horror the people of Oklahoma City experienced? Certainly sin is an essential category in the quest to comprehend. The theological perspectives I have outlined surely contain some insight into the meanings and motivations of human wrongdoing. Nevertheless, even when we have done our best to explain what sin is and how it comes about, a mystery of iniquity will remain that baffles the intellect. We will still be left wondering why people hurt and destroy each other the way they do. We can never probe the inner depths of the heart and the mind sufficiently to learn what leads human beings to bring such misery upon so many people in this and other cases of wickedness that plague our world. But even if we could exhaust the meaning of sin, we would require additional categories to assist us in exploring further dimensions of this atrocity. The categories of the demonic, the tragic, and the ambiguous can cast further light on what happened, but in the end the mind will not be satisfied. Nevertheless, such light as can be had is worth the effort.

---

1. For the thought of Irenaeus, Augustine, and Pelagius, see Jaroslav Pelikan, *The Christian Tradition* (Chicago: University of Chicago Press, 1971), I: 51, 144-145, 282-284, 299-301, 313-318. See also, J. N. D. Kelly, *Early Christian Doctrines*, 2nd ed. (New York: Harper & Row, 1960), 163-188, 344-374.

2. For further exposition and examples, see my *Systematic Theology: A Modern Protestant Approach* (Lewiston: The Edwin Mellen Press, 1986), 183-197, 222-223. For modern Pelagianism, see also my *The Impact of American Religious Liberalism* (New York: Harper & Row, 1962; Lanham, MD: University Press of America, 1983), 52-53, 76-77, 97-99, 118-120, 159-160, 181-183.

3. Reinhold Niebuhr, *The Nature and Destiny of Man*, One vol. ed. (New York: Charles Scribner's Sons, 1949), I:150-300.

4. See John Hick, *Evil and the God of Love* (San Francisco: Harper & Row, 1978), 199-364. Hick provides the strongest and most systematic statement of the Irenaean outlook, but aspects and elements of it may be found in a wide variety of ancient and contemporary thinkers.

5. "Moral evil is the tragic implication of creaturely freedom." Paul Tillich, *Systematic Theology*, 3 vols. (Chicago: University of Chicago Press, 1951, 1957, 1963), I:269.

6. *Ibid.*, I:67; II:19-44, 55-57; III:11-12.

7. Form and pattern are certainly present in things. In nature (apples, galaxies, dinosaurs, etc.), they are probably temporally emergent and exist only in the

entities themselves. Structures in concrete beings are not enactments of pre-existing, eternal, transhistorical ideals. In human artifacts (houses, computers, chairs, etc.), form and pattern are humanly invented. Or so I believe. I am impressed with the nominalist arguments against the notion of eternal essences that have been made against every effort to assert and defend them from Plato's forms or ideas to Whitehead's eternal objects. Should we explain similarities by universals or vice versa? Which forms are eternal and which are emergent? Whether there are any primordial material/energy elements (the original "stuff" from which all else was made) or some eternal necessities or inexorable laws that precede all particular cosmic developments and govern the emergence of particular forms of beings/processes, I do not know. Possibility in general does seem to just be in some original sense, but what the ontological status of mere possibility is, I do not know. I am agnostic about what Whitehead calls "the primordial nature of God." All particular patterns resident in particular things may emerge from some indeterminate matrix of possibility to become the form of concrete actualization, as Charles Hartshorne suggests. My brief speculations can be found in *Theological Biology*, 233-239.

8. See Judith Plaskow, *Sex, Sin and Grace: Women's Experience and the Theologies of Reinhold Niebuhr and Paul Tillich* (Washington: University Press of America, 1980).

9. Reinhold Niebuhr brilliantly recognizes that the social location and power status of individuals and groups can be correlated with different forms of sinful practice. Nevertheless, all this variety seems to be an expression primarily of pride and secondarily of sensuality. Niebuhr is an essentialist on sin. He offers a normative description, sets forth a paradigm, gives a standard example of its basic and essential features in its full-grown expression. For example, he says little about the origin of moral consciousness either in the evolutionary process or in the experience of children. Hence, he might admit that not all particular persons or instances of sin perfectly exemplify the essential or normative features he makes central to his analysis. See *The Nature and Destiny of Man*, I:186-240.

10. My understanding of the human situation is indebted most to Reinhold Niebuhr, *The Nature and Destiny of Man* (New York: Charles Scribner's Sons, 1949), I:150-300. However, in recent years, my views have increasingly taken markedly different directions from his. He would doubtless fault me for falling into a form of Pelagianism that excessively roots wrongdoing in nature rather than in spirit, in finitude rather than freedom. I in turn am convinced that the existentialism and Augustinianism he represents neglect the grounding of spirit in a biological substratum of energies and impulses that influences, though it does not determine, the self in its choices. Wrongdoing proceeds from nature and spirit.

11. I have already acknowledged the validity of the feminist claim that self-exaltation may be the more typical transgression of men, while self-depreciation is more characteristic of women. Numerous questions arise. Gender dissimilarities in moral failure, as well as in ethical reasoning and virtue, may be rooted in biology. Primordially, more similarity is likely between the sexes than is evident in present experience. I am not convinced that women are at heart free from tendencies toward self-glorification when the means to lord it over others are at hand, although men may be more innately inclined toward aggression and violence than women.

Chapter Five

Injustice And The Demonic: Dealing With Unfairness And Getting Free From Bondage

"I don't care what the Bible says." He spoke in anger and exasperation. Still it was disturbing to hear a deacon in a Baptist church say these words. He, of course, did care. He was driven to this outburst by the frustration he felt. He had come to tell me that the deacons wanted to have a meeting. He refused to call it without inviting me. It seems that some of the brothers and sisters wanted to remove me from the pastorate of the church I had served for nearly two years. He chaired the Board of Deacons, and his integrity would not allow a gathering in my absence. With heavy heart he had come to tell me the purpose of the meeting and to invite me to be present. The uproar had come about because I had written some letters to the Atlanta newspapers and had preached a sermon that marked me as an integrationist. This was not a popular position in the prevailing climate in those days in rural Georgia. The surrounding issue was the 1954 decision of the Supreme Court outlawing segregation in the public schools.

When he advised me of the movement to have me ousted, a long and fruitless argument ensued. We quarrelled about the wisdom of what I had done in my letters and in the more recent sermon. The greater offense, according to him, was the letters. They advertised to the world what a deviant thinker occupied the pulpit in their town. It put the membership in a bad light, he said.

I defended myself by an appeal to Scripture. "Show me on the basis of the Bible that I am wrong," I remonstrated, "and I will take it all back." I thought this would clinch the argument, or at least shift attention away from me to exegesis of the Book. Was I ever wrong! For it was then that this Baptist deacon startled me by saying, "I don't care what the Bible says; we are not going to permit our schools to be integrated!"

Before me stood a good man, a faithful Christian, admired and held in high esteem by everyone in that little town. He was the sort of person you would like to have as a neighbor. He would go out of his way to help you, regardless of your color. He was kind, considerate, friendly, and generous to a fault. He was old enough to be my father. I knew he loved me like a son. And I loved him. When it came to his attention that I had used a lot of gasoline doing my pastoral visitation to the sick in the community and in the Atlanta hospitals, he would quietly call me aside and invite me to stop by the station he ran for a free fill-up. Above all his integrity was beyond question. He was Chair of the deacons. He believed the Holy Word of God with all his heart. Yet here he was saying to the preacher who had angered him, "I don't care what the Bible says!"

This episode serves well as an introduction to two forms of social evil: injustice and the demonic. Segregation was an injustice because its effect was to deny to African-Americans the benefits to which they were entitled as human beings in the society to which they belonged and which their labors had helped to create. The commitment to segregation as a way of life also illustrated the power and the presence of the demonic. Both injustice and the demonic are evils that arise in the interconnectedness of individuals to each other in society and over the generations. With this introduction let me proceed to a more formal analysis.

INJUSTICE

Individuals are both relatively autonomous and deeply interdependent as they play out their social roles.[1] Our actions are configured by the prevailing institutions in ways that feed into a systemic whole that may have consequences we neither intend nor can prevent or escape. My lawfully buying grapes may contribute to the support of a system oppressive to migrant workers thousands of miles away. On the other hand, we can in limited ways make choices that to some degree decrease the destructive effects of institutional patterns and contribute to reform. I may along with others boycott grapes to put pressure on producers and lobby for legislation to benefit the workers. Beyond that individuals can choose to refuse to cooperate with social institutions and practices and join reform or revolutionary groups to bring about systemic change. Nevertheless, some of our actions will always have unwanted and unintended evil consequences when channelled through social structures as we live out our lives as citizens and workers in our everyday roles. It is impossible to live a completely pure life that does no evil to anyone. As Reinhold Niebuhr pointed out, even Jesus could incarnate perfect love only by becoming powerless on the cross, symbolically and literally lifted above the ambiguities and complexities of interconnected life in society.[2]

Injustice refers to the deprivation of rights, privileges, and opportunities to which persons have a rightful claim as free and equal members of society. It is the denial of the personal and social goods to which we are entitled. Injustice is itself one form of suffering. It denies the enjoyment that comes from full participation in a community to which ideally we contribute according to our abilities and receive according to our just claims.[3] Injustice is not the mere sum total of the actions of individuals acting wrongfully against their neighbors. It is also manifested in the institutions and patterns of social life. Racial, ethnic, and cultural minorities, along with women and the poor, are especially subject to deep-rooted, long-standing prejudices that pollute the social atmosphere and rob them as individuals and as groups of opportunities and benefits. Society is nearly always organized in ways that systemically help some and unfairly harm others, even when individuals act lawfully within the given structures. Even in democracies, the rich and powerful repeatedly manage to arrange things through money and influence so that the outcome of transactions within the social system preserves and promotes their interests. They are often aided and abetted by the moderately well off who believe (perhaps rightly) they have more to gain in prestige, psychic identity, or economic advantages by becoming the allies of the elite than by identifying with the plight of the poor, the lower classes, and the outcasts. As long as they are doing well, those in the broad center cannot be easily enlisted massively on the side of the worst off, since the changes necessary to eradicate poverty and primary need fully would be costly to the middle class as well as to the wealthy. In matters relating to race, gender, ethnic identity, culture, religion, and nationality, people of all classes may unite against their counterparts.

The varieties and sources of injustice are too numerous to outline here. Oppression takes a multitude of forms peculiar to given societies. The worst expressions involve the coercive and cruel subjugation of certain groups and individuals to the interests and aims of others who have the power to impose their will with impunity. No one has analyzed the social evils of modern industrial societies and the conflicts among nation-states more profoundly than Reinhold Niebuhr. However, in his preoccupation with the complexities and ambiguities of collective evil, he neglected the positive moral force exerted on individuals by group standards (or gave the impression he did). Societies are generally more moral in the norms and values they seek to inculcate in their citizens than are some members of the group. It is in their relationship to other collectives that races, classes, and nations are often more immoral than many of the individuals who compose them. Many individuals and subgroups may live by ideals that are superior to generally accepted standards. Societies tend to punish those whose behavior is too far below its rules and approved practices (sinners and criminals) and those who live too high above them (prophets and saints) when they challenge the established order of things. Jesus is an example of the latter; the thieves crucified with him exemplify the former. It is in their relationship to each other that races, classes, religious groups, and nations may be more immoral than the average of the individuals who compose them.[4]

THE DEMONIC

The category of the demonic is complex. In the background is the myth of superhuman or non-human bad spirits who produce suffering and evil in human affairs but whose own fallenness is a product originally of their own choice. The New Testament is replete with references to demonic powers.[5] In this essay the demonic refers to a structural power of evil originating in the past and operating effectively and systemically in human life and history in the present. The demonic is the destructive power of the past living on in the present as a configuration of harmful influence. As such it constitutes a pattern of forces that functions in individuals, in institutions, and in societies to produce evil that may be beyond the simple or immediate capacity of individual free choice to avoid or overcome. Yet since the evil arises from the contingencies of human freedom and not from natural necessities, the demonic can be overcome, at least in part, because of the capacity of creative self-transcendence in human beings.[6]

Let us return to the story of the deacon who disavowed the authority of Scripture if it meant that segregation — that unjust system — had to go. The author of Ephesians in the New Testament provides a point of entry. The writer uses the imagery of battle between opposing forces to interpret situations like this. Believers are to put on the whole armor of God in order to resist the wiles of the devil. Then comes the crucial insight.

> *For we are not contending against flesh and blood, but against the principalities, against the powers, against the world rulers of this present darkness, against the spiritual hosts of wickedness in the heavenly places* (Ephesians 6:12 RSV).

For modern ears, the notion that bad spirits inhabit the heavens and do mischief on earth is strange. What can it mean for us?

I translate this reference to demonic powers into another idiom. The spiritual hosts of wickedness are destructive powers from the past living on to produce moral blindness or weakness that results in suffering and injustice. What we wrestle against is not bad invisible beings, not literal devils. Rather in this world we are enslaved by the continuing influence of those historical developments that create structural impediments to moral goodness.

83

Segregation was a social arrangement that deprived African-Americans of freedom and equality. It was an instrument of racial domination. The many creators of this order over long periods of time invented an ideology to make it sound good, to give it moral status. The deacon was under demonic influence. He did not invent those evil ideas and practices but inherited them along with the accent in his speech. The demonic power lived on as he appropriated the past and embraced these unjust ideas and institutions as his own. He did so not knowing how evil the system was, even though the evidence was plain for all to see. He did so not knowing he was being deceived, not realizing that what he accepted as good was demonic. Not only was he infected, so were most white people in his time and place.

The injustice of slavery and segregation could not have survived as long as they did if they had been thought to be wrong. White church and white state and white society were all seduced by the lie that one race is better than another. In effect all conspired to promote the evil while calling it good. The power of these forces from the past was as real as literal devils. Moral blindness is a disease passed silently on from generation to generation. At last it afflicted the present generation. White Christians defended segregation under the illusion that they were innocent in doing so. So deeply enslaved were they by the evil powers that one of their number could say, "I don't care what the Bible says." That was the biggest lie of all.

The demonic enslaves people to perverse habits and excites and intensifies the potential for iniquity inherent in the human situation. Evil destructiveness originates in freedom united with destiny (given circumstances) and becomes a demonic power when it becomes embodied in personality structure and in social practices with tragic consequences. In these incarnate forms the demonic passes on from generation to generation. Those under its power may not be consciously aware that they are in bondage. The evil they suffer and the evil they do when demonically possessed is a tragic feature of their existence. The demonic as a structure cannot be willed away by a simple act of choice, although in individual cases it may be resisted. As a pattern of influence it must be exorcised through a process of liberation. It cannot be overcome by effortless, rational, moral decision making, since its victims are enslaved to the evil they do. Demonic possession may in a given situation be so effective as to weaken or even eliminate the capacity for the choice of good over evil. The demonic is worst of all when its expressions are called good, necessary, or even divinely sanctioned. Racism was and is a prime example of demonic forces at work in American history.

The evildoing that produces demonic structures arises in the past in the depths of the self preferentially oriented to its own good and excited by the imagined possibilities of self-aggrandizement in a context of anxious insecurity generated by the terrifying consciousness of finitude and mortality. Hence, contemplation of the future may fill us with dread. Anxiety is compounded by ignorance. Anxiety tempts the self toward egocentric actions to protect and fortify the self and thus to reduce existential dread, but freedom ratifies and exacerbates the urge.[7] Original evil, then, is the product of finitude and freedom experienced as the fascinating enticement of inordinate self-love that leads to destructive consequences.

The forms of the demonic are many and diverse. It may be experienced by individuals as a compulsion or possession, an irresistible urge toward destructive actions known to be so and contrary to conscious intent. It may take the form of neurotic or criminal behavior springing from unknown unconscious forces rooted deeply in early childhood experiences. Parents who were abused as children may, despite their conscious intention, abuse their own. Individuals socialized into unjust social systems may in willing or invincible ignorance perpetuate them without ever being conscious of their demonic nature. Moreover, social systems may themselves be ambiguous, producing both creative and destructive results.

Seldom is evil deliberately done for its own sake but most often results from some idolatrous or overzealous or misguided pursuit of what is at least partly good. Circumstances shape but do not determine human decisions, although they may in some extreme cases. For example, slavery flourished in the South because of geographical and climatic conditions aided and abetted by the invention of the cotton gin — all of which combined to make cotton growing profitable and to generate support of slavery from nature (following Aristotle) and by divine sanction (following Scripture). Wherever the demonic manifests itself, it creates a bondage that produces evil in individual and communal life. Yet since it originates in freedom, it can be overcome through freedom, but only through liberating experiences of grace in which the destructive power of the past is recognized in the presence of alternatives whose promise of new life energizes choice and generates structural transformation.

The demonic is essential to the understanding of some of the worst evils that occur in individual and collective life. Susan Smith took her two young children down by a lakeside in South Carolina. She strapped them in their car seats and pushed the car into the water. Both were drowned. At first she peddled a wild tale about how an African-American man had abducted the children and drove away with them. Later, she confessed that she had done this evil thing to her own children. What twisted motives or perverted thoughts led her in a moment of desperation to think that killing these two little boys could in any way be a solution to her problems? What inner rage, frustrations, and hatreds born in her past experiences could have taken over her rational faculties and overwhelmed her moral sensibilities so completely that she could bring herself to commit this despicable deed?

We may never know all the relevant facts of her short life or what choices she made in response to her traumatic past that resulted in her own ruin and the destruction of two small children. The fact that her father committed suicide when Susan was six years old shortly after he and her mother had divorced undoubtedly is an important factor in shaping her character. She made an attempt to take her own life when she was thirteen and did so again five years later. It is reasonable to assume that she was possessed by some pernicious influences rooted in her own past that blinded her to the meaning of her murderous act and fascinated her irresistibly with the vile possibility that she proceeded to turn into fact when she killed her children. Yet we cannot rule out the extent to which this heinous crime was the personal creation of Susan Smith in that present moment rather than the consequence of demonic possession. We cannot always know for sure in particular instances the extent to which the demonic is at work or whether some awful sinful choice freshly originates evil out of the depths of a self-perverted human heart.

Susan Smith took deliberate action to kill her two young boys. In another state two little children died because of their mother's negligence and carelessness. Jennie Bain of McMinnville, Tennessee, was charged with leaving her young sons, the oldest not yet quite two years old, strapped in a hot car with the windows rolled up. Temperatures rose to at least 120 degrees, authorities said. The boys died from hyperthermia, overheating. She had entered a motel about 3:30 a.m. that morning to party with four males who had once been her coworkers in a factory. The little children, buckled in their car seats, remained in the car for ten hours. While she had checked on them periodically, apparently she fell asleep later on and left them unattended long enough for the heat of the day to kill them. Was this an act of pure negligence and carelessness on this occasion unrelated to her past life? Or had her own previous bad choices and a destructive life history created a pattern of irresponsible living that she had difficulty resisting? Was there a structural impediment in her character that operated as an evil, enslaving influence that played a part in her irresponsibility that day? We cannot know the extent to which past influences not of her own creation and habits born out of her own freedom combined to produce neglect that killed her children.

The identifying feature of the demonic that separates it from simple evil is that it is a persisting structural impediment in the personality or character structure of an individual or a systemic distortion of a social institution or practice. When it is present, the demonic factor constitutes an evil influence on those who come under its sway. Its vile allure may range from blinding people to the wrong they unintentionally do to being an irresistible impulse that impels people under a spell of fascination to do deliberately what otherwise would be unthinkable. Generations of white southerners accepted segregation and white supremacy doctrines as right, proper, and decent, never questioning what they were taught from infancy onward. They were oblivious to the evils of the system and the lies told in its support, although the evidence was plain to the liberated eye. Pedophiles and serial killers perform their evil work as the expression of a systematically distorted personality structure that overwhelms clear moral insight and normal inhibitions against doing violence to the innocent. In all cases the capacity to know and to do good and to avoid evil is hampered. The demonic tends to create a habit of evildoing in an individual or to weave a pattern of destructive values and practices into the culture that perniciously influences every new generation. Homophobia born of ignorance, cultural conditioning, and vague anxieties related to the alleged weirdness, unnatural character, and viscerally felt taboo associated with same-sex love must surely qualify as an example of demonic evil. Objective rational inquiry will not sustain the hatreds shown toward those who represent the sexually different — the threatening other who must be feared, repressed, and even destroyed.

The evils perpetrated during the Nazi era in Germany defy understanding unless we have recourse to the explanatory power of the demonic. Out of the chaos following World War I in Germany was born a movement led by Adolf Hitler that was destined to fill the world with blood, hate, and violence. The German leader was able to mobilize the frustrations, prejudices, felt injustices, and legitimate aspirations widespread among the masses into a powerful program promising liberation and national glory but that led to giant agonies and massive ruin. At the heart of the Nazi campaign were fatal distortions of truth and a fanatical glorification of blood and soil that produced disaster.

The Holocaust that destroyed six million Jews is only the most vivid symbol of the atrocities and horrors flowing from the ethnic and national idolatry that aroused hatred toward all who did not fit the Aryan standard of race and culture. A devilish power of monstrous proportions was unleashed in which truth, justice, and decency were systemically perverted in a creed that seduced millions of people into believing in the nobility of the Nazi cause. A leading philosopher of religion in this country indicated his belief that Germany would not resort to a Hitler or long tolerate a dictatorship because of the high educational standards that prevailed there![8] How easy it is to underestimate the power of the demonic in wreaking havoc on earth among those who presumably might be least susceptible to its wiles.

Daniel Day Williams tells about a young woman engaged to a German storm trooper who reports the excitement she felt in the early days of National Socialism. At a youth rally on the Rhine in the spring she is caught up in the delirium of the crowd and her own sense of commitment. She says, "A desire began to burgeon within me, to be permitted to help, like these women and girls in the great work of our leader, Adolf Hitler." She was trancelike in expectation of the evening assembly. There was the campfire, the songs, the prayers, the fervent speech by Hermann Goering. "The rustle of the Rhine sounds like a prayer for redemption from foreign despotism." Goering stood in the circle around the fire. She held a torch over his shoulder lighting up his face for the crowd to see. "Who could have been happier than I?"[9]

The demonic fascinates, excites, blinds, charms, possesses, entices to action, and generates fanatical passion. In the Nazi cause all was done in the interest of a perceived good that was in fact cunning evil in disguise. Nothing but an inner structural perversion of ideas, symbols, and values can account for the Hitler years. Demonic power was incarnate in great historical forces enslaving the minds and hearts of masses of people caught up in a situation that threatened doom but promised redemption if the moment were seized. Freedom and destiny, choice and circumstance, personal decision and historical fate unite in the creation and spread of demonic infection within individual lives and throughout a whole culture over time.

On November 4, 1995, Yigal Amir shot and killed Yitzhak Rabin. A longtime soldier, the Prime Minister of Israel was leaving a rally in Tel Aviv where he had been singing songs of peace. The 25-year-old law student said that he murdered Mr. Rabin in obedience to Jewish religious law. God, he claimed, inspired him to kill the leader of Israel who was negotiating a peace settlement with the Arabs. Because in the process he was promising to give up land that was believed to have been given them by God long ago, the Prime Minister had in the eyes of some Jewish extremists become a traitor who deserved death. All the elements that produce the demonic were here. A complicated past filled with conflict and hate had poisoned the present with virulent attitudes. In this atmosphere a young man, inheriting and reproducing malice arising out of a tragic history he did not create, could claim divine guidance in committing murder. He assassinated a person who had said, "Enough of blood and tears!" Yigal Amir murdered a leader who had dedicated himself to achieving reconciliation with ancient enemies against whom he himself had led armies into war. On the lawn of the White House in Washington, D.C., as television cameras beamed pictures around the world, Yitzhak Rabin had shaken the hand of Yasser Arafat, the leader of the Palestinian Liberation Organization, as they made a mutual pledge to end the violence between Jews and Arabs. For this and other acts of peacemaking, the demonic did its monstrous work through Yigal Amir to produce a killing that caused the world to mourn for a lost peacemaker and Noa Ben Artzi to weep bitter tears as she said a sad farewell to her beloved grandfather.

Was a tangled web of demonic powers involved in the outrage at Oklahoma City? Soon after this event we heard of extremist paramilitary groups full of hatred against the government who train with guns for a battle sure to come. They are suffused with paranoia about mostly imagined threats on the basis of bizarre interpretations of events current and past. In particular, the fiery end to the Branch Davidian compound in Waco, Texas, involving federal authorities confirms in their eyes their preposterous outlook. In this devilish stew are doubtless combined other ingredients to create a fanaticism beyond the reach of reason to persuade otherwise.[10] The alleged perpetrators of the bombing at Oklahoma City appear to be of this ilk but too radical even for the organized militia groups themselves. Much is still unknown, but we can almost predict that the guilty parties were poisoned somewhere along the way by lies and distortions that evoked their own consent. Surely they were blinded by seductive influences not entirely of their own making that spring ultimately from perverted choices that led to a dreadful sickness of mind and spirit.

In so far as grotesque choices were made in the past by themselves or others that set in motion or contributed to a structured sequence of destructive events, the tragic destiny they now live out is demonic in character. For it would certainly appear that their own rationality and wills became enslaved to evil chimeras that made them immune to normal inhibitions against violence of such proportions. Did past influences originating in sinful actions enter into the formation of a depraved personality structure capable of breeding rancorous, baleful violence? What was their family life like particularly in the early years? What was their life like at home, at school, at work? Were they unloved, abused, hated, neglected, persecuted, made to feel they were trash? Has the past given them reason to fear enemies who would destroy them? Is their hate some form of self-protection from a painful history and the dread of destruction from some imagined foe? Only an intimate and detailed knowledge of the lives of these doomed souls could give particulars to these speculative questions.[11] It is not unreasonable, however, to suspect the presence of the demonic at work in the horror of the Oklahoma City bombing.

Risk is always involved in identifying the demonic. For what suggests satanic seduction to one may symbolize angelic inspiration to another. Often it is only looking back from a liberated future that the power of the demonic can be seen clearly. Witness the belated recognition of Gov. George Wallace of Alabama that he had been wrong about segregation. Let us give him the benefit of the doubt and consider his repentance genuine, notwithstanding the fact that it became politically expedient for him to seek black votes. The Southern Baptist Convention in its 1995 meeting in Atlanta confessed to the sin of racism in its complicity with slavery and segregation. Consider the former Defense Secretary Robert McNamara as he writes three decades later that the Vietnam War was "wrong, terribly wrong." Was it mere ignorance and bad judgment on the part of "the brightest and the best" (David Halberstam) of American leaders that led to the Vietnam debacle, or was wisdom systemically perverted by inherited myths about Communism, the asinine excesses of the continuing cold war, and the overweening expressions of nationalistic pride? Most German people today acknowledge in sorrow the evils of the Nazi period. Courage is required to take the risk of identifying and opposing the demonic in the light of the best we know up to now.

The demonic and the tragic are often interwoven with each other. What is demonic in the malefactors means tragedy for them and tragedy for the victims as well. The demonic originates in choice or involves an element of choice among the factors that generate and sustain its destructive power. The tragic refers to suffering its victims cannot avoid or redeem. To this we now turn.

----

1. Some material in this section is taken from my *Theological Biology* (Lewiston: Edwin Mellen Press, 1991), 260-262, with some revisions and additions.

2. See Reinhold Niebuhr, *The Nature and Destiny of Man,* (New York: Charles Scribner's Sons, 1949), II:35-97.

3. See my *Process Ethics: A Constructive System* (Lewiston: The Edwin Mellen Press, 1984), and *The Passion for Equality* (Totowa, NJ: Rowman & Littlefield, 1987), for extensive discussions of the meaning of justice.

4. This is to say that the relationship between the morality of individuals and of groups is more complex than appeared in Niebuhr's early work *Moral Man and Immoral Society* (New York: Charles Scribner's Sons, 1932). See also, *The Nature and Destiny of Man* and *Faith and History* (New York: Charles Scribner's Sons, 1949), as well as most any of his other numerous works on economic, social, and political forms of injustice.

5. See, for example, Mk. 5:1-18, 9:17-29; Rom. 8:38-39; 1 Cor. 2:2-8, 15:24-28; 2 Cor. 5:17; Eph. 1:3-2:10, 6:10-20; Phil. 2:9-11; Col. 1:13-20, 2:8-20; 2 Thess. 2:3-12; Heb. 2:10-18; 1 Pet. 5:8-10; Rev. 20-21.

6. See my *Theological Biology*, 173-174. I have been influenced by Tillich's understanding of the demonic as "a 'structure of evil' beyond the moral power of good will, producing social and individual tragedy precisely through the inseparable mixture of good and evil in every human act." *The Protestant Era* (Chicago: University of Chicago Press, 1948), xx-xxi. See also "The Demonic" in *The Interpretation of History* (New York: Charles Scribner's Sons, 1936), and Daniel Day Williams, *The Demonic and the Divine* (Minneapolis: Fortress Press, 1990). Finally, see the notion of "superpersonal powers of evil" in Walter Rauschenbusch, *A Theology for the Social Gospel* (New York: The Macmillan Co., 1917), chapters VIII and IX.

7. My understanding of the human situation is indebted most to Reinhold Niebuhr, *The Nature and Destiny of Man,* I:150-300. Niebuhr here sets forth his views regarding the origin of sin (original sin). In my view, the demonic is closely related to sin, but refers specifically to the incarnation of sinful acts in the past into structural forms that are transmitted from generation to generation in behavioral patterns of individuals and in social institutions and practices.

8. Eugene W. Lyman, *The Meaning and Truth of Religion* (New York: Charles Scribner's Sons, 1933), 443-444.

9. Williams, *The Demonic and the Divine*, 7.

10. See Garry Wills, "The New Revolutionaries," *The New York Review of Books* (August 10, 1995), 50-55.

11. We know some of the details of the troubled lives and traumas of Timothy McVeigh and Terry Nichols, both allegedly involved in the bombing. Both men, e.g., experienced a parental divorce and a disturbed family and work history in the midst of declining economic opportunity for blue-collar workers. See Dale Russakoff and Serge F. Kovaleski, "Two Angry Men," *The Washington Post National Weekly Edition* (July 24-30, 1995), 6-11. I assert no causal connection here. Thousands of other young men have had similar life histories but would never commit such a horrendous act. The crucial and defining moments in the deep recesses of the inner spirit of these two people in response to the external events of their lives are closed to our view.

Chapter Six

The Tragic And The Ambiguous: Unavoidable Suffering, Irredeemable Loss, And Good Inseparable From Evil

The words stabbed me in the heart. They come back to me again and again. It was nearly twenty years ago. I sat in the Detroit airport with a couple of hours of waiting before my plane for Rochester departed. I bought a newspaper to pass the time. In an advice column I came across this letter:

> *Dear Jane Lee: I am an adult who was, and still am, despised and ridiculed because I am ugly ... I have a rock bottom opinion of myself. I've never had a friend. In school, my classmates used to torment me with their cruelties ... When I went to work, I was harassed by cruel taunts ... My husband doesn't have any feeling for me. He would have left long ago if he could have afforded it. He said once — at a time when I was pregnant with one of our children — that my face turns his stomach. I sure would like to earn some money to get an education and some of the nice things in life, but I am afraid to go any place because people stare or snicker ... I've never murdered anyone. I don't peddle drugs to the young. I've never stolen from others or slandered others. I do the best I can as a wife and mother ... I would have given up on life a long time ago, but somehow I keep looking for a rainbow.[1]*

What can we say to this poor soul who has suffered all her life because she is ugly? Our first response may be to assign responsibility to her for the way she reacts to the face she was born with. Maybe we want to admonish her sternly to stop wallowing in self-pity and do something about the situation. We quote that cute little platitude: If life deals you a lemon, make lemonade. Is that all we have to have to say? Do we hint that there must be some purpose in it, since God works for good in all things for those who believe (Romans 8:28)? Do we even suggest that suffering can be good for us, that it develops the soul? Do we quote again from Romans and urge her to rejoice in her suffering, since suffering leads through endurance to character and from character to hope (Romans 5:1-5)? Do we urge her to believe that God's grace is sufficient for every need? Beyond that, of course, in our psychologically oriented age, we might urge her to seek a secular doctor of the soul. Surely what she finally needs is a psychotherapist. But is that the end of it?

I do not want to rule out any of these responses. They all may have a point. Nevertheless, if this is all that can be said, I am a bit uneasy. All that has been said so far puts the responsibility back on the shoulders of that poor woman. We have said that if she will only get right with God and have enough faith, if only she will have the right attitude about it, see it in the proper light, come to terms with the facts, take charge of her life, lemons can become lemonade.

We seem so eager to get God off the hook. Either God has a purpose in it or will supply the grace that overcomes all. Or we are content to appeal to the mystery of God's ways of dealing with us. The assumption seems to be that the problem is finally all with her and not at all with the fact that she was born ugly. No, we say, the difficulty lies with all those people who have treated her terribly. That is not God's fault. Maybe, but what accounts for the fact that she was born ugly? But, we protest, ugly is a subjective judgment, a cultural matter. God is not to blame for that. Maybe, but we all have some notion in our heads about who is beautiful and who is not even if we act nicely toward everybody. No matter how long this sort of conversation goes on, I am left troubled.

THE TRAGIC

I want to pursue another line of thought. With heaviness of heart, I conclude that some suffering occurs that neither God nor the victims can fully overcome no matter how hard they struggle. We are limited in the extent to which we can triumph over evil either in fact or in our spirits. God too is limited and labors to overcome evil with only partial success.

I revolt against the old Calvinist doctrine of predestination. The thought that God has chosen from all eternity some people to be saved and some to be damned forever is getting close to the most horrible idea conceivable. Let us hope it is not true. Nevertheless, a remnant of truth may be contained in a reinterpreted version. It does appear that some people in this life are born to be damned in some if not all aspects of their lives. I mean that they suffer as the victim of circumstances or the actions of others over which they have no control.

A biography of Rita Hayworth appeared a few years ago. She was beautiful and glamorous in the movies. She will be remembered as the most famous pinup of World War II. It is an image that all of us old enough to recall have in our minds. She was married to some of the world's richest and most celebrated men. Yet the heading of the review in *The New York Times* reads: "What we have here is a very sad story." She was sexually abused by her father and exploited by him in terrible ways. At age twelve she sat fat and silent on her front porch staring straight ahead, afraid to play with other children. She lived through a lifetime of disastrous relationships and was manipulated and used by a succession of men. Her life deteriorated rapidly, punctuated by drinking sprees, irrational outbursts, and failing health. Her career disintegrated. At long last at age 62, she was diagnosed as being in an advanced stage of Alzheimer's disease. One redeeming note is that her daughter Yasmin became her legal guardian and took loving care of her until she died in 1987. I do not know all that is involved or how her own free will entered into the situation. It does appear that from early childhood on she was destroyed by powers over which she had limited control. She appears to have been damned from the start.

Listen to the stories of runaway children, of serial killers, of drug addicts and prostitutes. Look into the sad faces of starving babies in Africa. Consider the circumstances of those who populate the mental hospitals of the land for a lifetime, perpetually tormented in body and spirit. Hear the life histories of the homeless and destitute, those serving life sentences in prison. Whatever responsibility they have for their own destinies, I cannot escape the conclusion that an element of tragedy pervades it all. All around are people caught up, tossed about, mangled, and destroyed by forces over which they have limited control. One thirteen-year-old girl who had run away reported that she left home because her stepbrother had raped her. Her father told her he was going to have her raped anyway. In all this is an element of the tragic — suffering that the victims could not totally prevent, nor can they always or fully overcome it. Neither is it always possible for them to triumph spiritually over all adversity by the resources of divine grace. They are damned in body and spirit.

Let me stress again that I do not want to ignore or even to underplay the role that human beings themselves play in determining their destiny. Is anyone so molded by circumstances that he or she could not have altered the outcome in any shape, form, or fashion? I doubt it. We usually have a choice within some range of available options. Nor do I want to deny that some people do prevail spiritually over great obstacles. All I insist on is that there are limits to what we can do to prevent or to overcome the injustices, miseries, and calamities that beset us. What about that other part that determines our lives over which we have no control? Circumstances create a destiny that we live out. It is in that portion of life beyond the range of human decision to alter that tragedy resides.

I like to watch the weight lifters compete during the Olympics. Here are athletes who have trained long and hard to develop their strength to the highest degree possible. The time has come. They bend and lift. Every muscle strains and trembles. They sweat and groan. They push their bodies until they have exhausted their powers. No matter how much they lift, they always reach a limit beyond which they simply cannot go. The weight comes crashing down. This is my point about life. We don't always exert ourselves to the extreme frontier of our creative capacity to make the lemons of our lives into lemonade. Sometimes we do not conquer the demons that torment us because we give up too soon or don't try hard enough. Until we pass that line between unwilling and unable, the limit we cannot exceed, the terrible has not yet become the tragic. But some human suffering lies beyond the region over which we have control. At that point, we are in the hands of powers that flesh and blood cannot conquer.

In common parlance, tragedy is related to the magnitude, severity, and awfulness of distress and disaster. Moreover, tragedy suggests events that evoke sadness, melancholy, pity, and threaten despair. These usages are not eliminated here, but a more precise delineation is needed. My intention is to locate the center and the vicinity of the tragic, not to define precise or rigid boundaries.[2] The presupposition of tragic suffering is finitude, which makes us vulnerable in body and soul to disruption and destruction. Animals and human beings are organized systems whose healthy functioning depends on many parts properly working together. Hence, something can go wrong and to some extent in every life unavoidably does. The enjoyment of life and the quest for happiness under conditions of justice may be frustrated or facilitated by circumstances in our personal history, our family life, and our social environment over which we have little or no control. Tragedy and finitude are inextricably interwoven. More exactly, the presupposition of the tragic lies in the fact that the finitude of sentient beings necessarily entails the possibility of suffering. Actual suffering takes on a tragic dimension in a variety of circumstances. Empirically, the tragic revolves around two overlapping dimensions: unavoidability and irredeemability.[3]

(1) Suffering is tragic to the extent that it cannot be avoided by those who are hurt.[4] In the purest denotation tragedy is associated with inevitable outcomes. In this narrow sense it is the product of factors that operate inexorably to produce tribulation. In an extended sense a dimension of tragedy attaches to sorrow and woe that are unavoidable for those undergoing it but that do not result by necessity from given conditions. If certain natural contingencies

had been otherwise, or if perpetrators had chosen differently, tragedy would not ensue. Self-inflicted tragedy may occur contrary to intent when no negligence is involved. Self-hurt as a result of carelessness may be serious but not tragic. If a swimmer dives into a shallow body of water and breaks her/his neck and becomes paralyzed for life from the neck down, the event is not — as awful as it is — tragic to the extent that it could have been prevented by forethought and caution. It is tragic because the injury is serious and permanent. Or self-hurt may be intentional in situations in which those involved lack the resources to do differently. A person who commits suicide may do so deliberately (intentionally) but in that awful moment of distress and despair may not be capable of doing otherwise (unavoidably). Self-inflicted tragic outcomes may result from personal deficiency or from flaws or contradictions in character.

When inflicted by nature or other people, tragic suffering is undeserved but beyond the power of the victim to prevent or overcome. The experience of injustice is a type of suffering. Suffering that is the consequence of enslavement to demonic powers is tragic. The tragic may arise out of ambiguities or contradictions in the historical circumstances that constrain our choices. Sometimes justice or a net gain in some good for some cannot be achieved except by causing undeserved loss for others. Finally, tragic suffering may result from our genetic inheritance, accidents, disease, tornadoes, and the like, i.e., spring from nature rather from history. The tragedy we experience is our destiny, but it may be compounded, transformed, or limited by freedom.

By extension the tragic refers not only to suffering that is unavoidably undergone but also to evil that is unavoidably done. This could involve accidental harm to others where neither bad intention nor carelessness was involved. Tragic also are those instances in which people have lost the capacity to avoid evildoing because of a life history that has destroyed their capacity to exercise moral freedom. While most people retain some capacity to distinguish good and evil and to choose between them, the possibility of a near total obliteration of moral ability cannot be ruled out. The result is tragic both for them and for the victims of their depravity.

(2) Suffering is tragic to the extent that it is pointless and irredeemable. Tragic suffering is meaningless and purposeless. It cannot be made into something different. An evil may seem to be senseless but acquire meaning by the way some or all who are affected respond. Over a period of time misery may result in good consequences hardly conceivable apart from some past affliction. A painful divorce may over time lead to reconciliation and a deepening of relationships among all involved that would or could not have occurred otherwise. In this sense the suffering caused by the marital breakup may be redeemed to a significant degree. To the contrary, a permanent loss of sight is tragic as such in that a valuable capacity is gone beyond recovery, even though blindness may contribute to gains of other sorts that might not or even could not have occurred otherwise. Eyesight is valuable in itself, and other goods, no matter how precious in themselves, cannot substitute or compensate for it. Not all suffering, however, can be given meaning or made to serve a purpose and remains forever pointless for all concerned.

The possibility of loss, disruption, and destruction is the inevitable and inescapable implication of finitude. Finite existence and the likelihood of tragedy are by necessity inseparable. Actual suffering becomes tragic (1) when it is of serious magnitude, intensity, and duration and (2) when it involves empirical elements of unavoidability, pointlessness, and irredeemability.

I don't know what happened to that woman I read about in the Detroit airport who lived a dreadful life because she was ugly. I wonder whether she finally gave up or whether she found the rainbow she was looking for. After everything else is said, I want to say to her the following: "God knows, and God cares. God did not make you ugly for some hidden divine purpose. I believe the reason you were born ugly is not because God intended it but because God could not prevent it.[5] But God suffers with you in your agony. God shares your pain as one who has a hard time too. God has a heart with a scar in the shape of a cross. That heart is broken for you. God is working through your urge to live and find fulfillment to bring the best that is possible out of this situation. Do the best you can to cooperate with God to make that happen."

THE AMBIGUOUS

Life is a mixture of good and evil. Experience and observation keep that fact before us. Jesus told a story that illustrates the point. A farmer sowed good seed in his field. His enemy came by night and planted weeds among the wheat. Soon both were growing up together. The offending weed is apparently darnel, a grain that resembles wheat but is poisonous to eat. Shall an attempt be made to pull out the weeds? No, says the farmer, let them grow together until the harvest. Then a separation can be made. To pull up the weeds now would uproot some of the wheat as well.

The ambiguous refers to the presence of two (or more) opposing elements in a situation. As used here ambiguity refers to events or clusters of events in which good and evil are closely interconnected either as causes and effects of each other or as products of the same source. More narrowly, ambiguity refers to the inseparable mixture of good and evil in events and in choices. This kind of ambiguity cannot be overcome by freedom, but freedom may choose the better rather than the worse of the trade-offs and may redeem in whole or in part the evil consequences of unavoidable choices. Conflicts in values such that something good cannot be achieved without introducing evil along with it is part of the tragic nature of historical existence. Evil thus originated may exacerbate and perpetuate the demonic. Ambiguity also refers to the presence of truth and error in theories and statements.

Ambiguity appears in many guises, and not all forms are of the same logical type. In particular, we need to distinguish between (1) instances in which good and evil are intrinsically interconnected and thus inseparable and (2) instances in which good and evil are actually present together and closely related in the total situation but separable. In (1) you cannot have the good without the evil it is bound up with. In (2) it is possible in principle to have one without the other. The first we can call metaphysical ambiguity. The second we can call factual ambiguity. The former cannot be overcome by human choices and actions, while the latter can. Some problems in personal life and at the society level seem to combine elements of both. Many social policies may have the appearance of (1) in terms of the intertwining of good and evil, but with compromise and compensatory actions the good may be maximized and the evil minimized, if not totally eliminated.

Sometimes a present situation that is ambiguous in the sense of meaning (1) could have been avoided if preceding circumstance or choices had been different. An unfortunate past may create an emergency or crisis such that no matter what we do now, both good and evil will result. It should be possible to discern from the context in what follows the extent to which the intermixture of good and evil participates in these possibilities. Discerning when problems can be dealt with to achieve unequivocal good and when unambiguous results are impossible taxes our wisdom to the limit. Human creativity must be exercised to the fullest to meet the challenge of reaching the best compromise or devising a novel solution that maximizes the desirable and minimizes the unwanted.

Ambiguity, then, does not mean simply that good and evil are both present in the world. The deeper reality is that good and evil in some measure are dependent on the other. Often we cannot have one without the other. Well-intentioned actions that have pre-dominantly good consequences may unavoidably have others that are destructive, there being no choice that is wholly positive with no negative outcomes. Some prescription drugs that do much good have unwanted side effects that can be serious. The same is true of many moral prescriptions. Even the purest of moral aims cannot change this fact. Ambiguous also is the connectedness among human beings that unites our individual sorrows as well as our joys. Sharing the joys and triumphs of those we love is one of life's sweetest pleasures, but when disaster or failure strikes them, our hearts bleed too. In all these cases, we cannot have the roses without the thorns. A few examples will illustrate the point further.

RELIGION

Hardly any aspect of our common life is more ambiguous than religion. Religious faith offers comfort and hope in the midst of the trials and troubles of this life and often generates moral energy to heal the wounds of the suffering and to bring about justice in the social order. Yet those same religious people and institutions often have claimed the approval of God for nearly every evil the world has known. We only need to mention the role of religion in defending slavery and segregation and the subjugation of women in the past. In the present gays and lesbians, no matter how responsible their love affairs may be, are condemned with quotations from the Bible and the Pope. Roman Catholic piety produces good works that aid the hungry, the poor, and the helpless, but official Roman Catholic doctrine makes the most effective forms of birth control a sin and denies the priesthood to women. The Religious Right in its zeal to preserve traditional values surrounding sex, marriage, and the family conspires with conservative politicians to support policies inimical to the interests of minorities, women, homosexuals, and the poor. Southern Baptists, who nurtured me spiritually during my early years, exhibited a zeal that sent missionaries around the world to preach the Gospel, feed the hungry, and heal the sick. Yet at home for decades they would not receive into their own fellowship believers from Africa who had been converted under their own ministries.

Religious fanatics at the fringes, fervent in their devotion, have no hesitation in cutting off the heads of their enemies in the name of God. Religious extremists in every religion resort to terrorism and violence to achieve ends believed to be divinely authorized. Pacifists may allow cruel tyrants to oppress the weak, since the only effective resistance is forbidden by a commitment to nonviolence. Just war theorists may authorize wars that achieve their relatively good ends only by inflicting death on the enemies of justice. The list could go on.

Is religion intrinsically and unavoidably ambiguous? Would not good religion be wholly on the side of the angels? The historic world religions advocate and inspire love and compassion in every generation. Religious faith is often allied with justice. The ideal possibilities for religion on earth if enacted would obviously eliminate much of the ambiguity that actual practice now exhibits. The deeper truth, however, may have been captured by Reinhold Niebuhr. He noted that Jesus himself could incarnate perfect love only by becoming powerless on the cross, symbolically and literally lifted above the ambiguities and complexities of interconnected life in society.[6] The point is that the exercise of power in actual life with all its interrelatedness is apt to have ambiguous consequences that produce evil in the pursuit of good or generate good while committing evil.

ANGRY WHITE MEN AND CULTURAL LIBERALS

Ambiguities abound in the economic and political order. Consider the "angry white men" who resist the struggle of African-Americans, women, gays, lesbians, and other groups for full equality and inclusiveness in American society. This obstinacy cannot be condoned. Yet many of them have been squeezed unmercifully by changes in the national and global economy that reduce the availability of high-paying jobs for those with limited education and few skills.[7] At the same time they feel threatened as they see aspects of traditional morality they were taught to honor under attack in the culture, especially values having to do with religion, sex, marriage, and family. These economic stresses and moral anxieties provide fertile ground for exploitation by politicians. Promising to get tough on crime, end affirmative action, limit welfare benefits, put recipients to work, protect "family values," and put prayer back into schools, conservative and reactionary office seekers garner their votes. Unfortunately, these would-be saviors of white males sponsor economic policies that result in a redistribution of income upward to corporate elites and the affluent. These strategies run contrary to the interests of many in the middle class as well as the poor and working classes that include many of these very same "angry white men."[8]

Meanwhile, many middle and upper middle-class cultural liberals who crave a more open, tolerant, and inclusive society favorable to the interests of previously oppressed groups are so turned off by the traditionalism and reactionary moral attitudes of the white working classes that they tend to be insensitive to the genuine economic distress of these offended males. So accustomed are they to seeing working-class white males as victimizers of their favorite victims, it is hard for them to appreciate the fact that working-class white men can also be victims of societal forces beyond their control. So interwoven are the complexities, contradictions, and ambiguities of class, race, gender, and cultural outlook that it is nearly impossible to combine into one political agenda capable of attracting an electoral majority all that a comprehensive justice might require.[9]

ECONOMIC ISSUES

The economy is a veritable breeding ground of ambiguities.[10] We have long been accustomed to the trade-off between inflation and unemployment. Measures that reduce one tend to increase the other, but we want both low inflation and high employment. More recently we hear about the tension between keeping inflation down and stimulating economic growth. Periodically, the question of the minimum wage becomes a matter of controversy, most recently in 1996. One side maintains that raising it will improve the lot of entry level workers who cannot support themselves or a family decently on the present wage rates that many people get stuck in these days. The other side argues that the consequence of increasing wages by law will be a loss of employment for a significant number of people. As business people find themselves unable to compete when their labor costs are raised beyond what the market will bear, they will fire workers. The evidence is not unequivocal, but it does appear that some sort of trade-off is present. We would like to raise wages for those who would be most helped, but the price may be some loss of employment for those who badly need jobs. According to Nobel Prize-winning economist Robert Solow, a panel of economists at the American Economics Association, meeting in January, 1996, concluded that "the employment effect of a moderate increase in the minimum wage would be very, very small."[11] But the debate continues with no resolution in sight.

PUBLIC QUANDARIES

Other ambiguities relate to the tension between individual liberty, the rights of others, and the common good. Sometimes the commitment to free speech entails the defense of unsavory characters whose use of liberty may be offensive both to justice and to good taste. College communities wanting to protect minorities from "hate" speech may find that the only way to do it is to ban "free" speech. Efforts to produce greater equality of income and opportunity for less fortunate citizens may require governmental coercion that infringes upon the liberty of others.[12] Zealous and long-range testing of new drugs may keep them off the market while people who need them die needlessly, but the same cautious policies may prevent another thalidomide tragedy. Raising speed limits on interstate highways may have a variety of benefits, but it may increase the number who die in accidents.

How far should we go in regulating tobacco even though the restrictions may limit the choice of smokers and do harm to farmers who grow it? Yet tobacco is responsible for hundreds of thousands of deaths each year and adds substantially to medical costs. The early death of smokers is a countervailing factor, of course, reducing the number of people who would otherwise claim social security benefits or need expensive care in old age! What rights does a community have to protect itself when a convicted sex-offender known for repeating the same crime is about to be released to live in the neighborhood? Are coercive efforts to trace the sources of HIV infection legitimated by concern for public health or are they merely an offense to individual liberty?

Unless we recognize the presence of ambiguity and complexity that mark many of our individual and political choices, we cannot find our way to wisdom. Meanwhile, opposing parties argue as if all truth and justice were totally on their side while their opponents persist stubbornly in their advocacy of pure falsehood and wrong.

AFFIRMATIVE ACTION

Affirmative action that helps women and minorities make up for past discrimination may in some cases be unfair to white males here and now considered as individuals. Under attack at the moment, affirmative action is frequently debated and reported in polls as if it meant just one thing and were a simple matter one needs to be either for or against, something that is either right or wrong, just or unjust. If we consider women and blacks as members of groups who have because of this identity been subject to past oppression, then remedies based on group membership are appropriate. Yet men and white people considered as individuals not responsible for the practices of former generations and not

107

themselves guilty of prejudice or discrimination in their own personal habits may be unfairly affected by policies that treat them on a group basis. Nevertheless, even though specific individual males or white people may not be guilty of racial or gender bias, they may have benefitted by their group status.

Ought we always to look at people as individuals, or is it sometimes legitimate, even obligatory, to treat persons in terms of their group membership, e.g., as women or as African-Americans or as Native Americans? Should the aim be to promote and ensure equal opportunity or to guarantee equal results? Does justice mandate race- and gender-neutral schemes or preferential treatment for previously oppressed groups? No policy option is without ambiguity.[13]

WELFARE AND POVERTY

What are we to do about poverty and welfare? To explore the issues, let us ask which of the following statements are true:

1. Payments to poor mothers with dependent children provide a safety net for families who have had the misfortune to fall on hard times temporarily.

2. Welfare queens, promiscuous teenagers, and lazy, deadbeat moms are living off hardworking taxpayers, while unreliable males father children and then escape responsibility.

3. A culture of poverty exists within the underclass that requires an individual, family, and community transformation of values and habits to improve their economic lot.

4. General economic and social conditions have created whatever pathologies may exist in the underclass, so that they are mainly society's fault.

5. Past government policies have created a culture of welfare dependency that is rotting the moral fabric of the destitute.

6. Reform measures that put work requirements or time limits on welfare recipients, place caps on payments, and refuse additional awards to mothers who keep having children are cruel measures that punish the poor, especially children.

7. Cutting off subsidies would be an incentive for mothers on welfare to have fewer babies.

8. Women have children for reasons hardly affected by having a little more or a little less welfare money.

9. The breakdown of two-parent families and the rise of births to non-married women are general cultural phenomena that have multiple causes not restricted to the poor and mostly unrelated to welfare policies.

10. Poor single mothers seek welfare because no jobs are available.

11. Poor single mothers prefer an easy monthly check to the discipline of work.

12. The available jobs they qualify for are mainly dead-end, low-paying, dull, and onerous. Many are at a distance from where they live.

13. Many poor single mothers lack competence, education, discipline, acceptable work habits, and self-confidence.

14. They need the goad of economic need to motivate them.

15. Counseling, training, child-care help, decent job openings, and encouragement would be sufficient to get many able-bodied poor mothers on a payroll and off the dole.

16. We can require personal responsibility from mothers without punishing innocent children if we provide assistance in job-training, job-seeking, child care, and other necessary services, but doing so would be more costly than sending them a check.

17. Putting welfare recipients to work is a good idea, but jobs are not always available in the private sector, and if the government provides subsidized work, powerful unions representing government workers will protest for fear of being displaced.

18. We can do what is humane for mothers and their children without making it easier for fathers to evade their duty.

19. Welfare payments to unwed mothers are an incentive to males to procreate while avoiding the financial disciplines of fatherhood.

20. Restricting or cutting off welfare payments to teenage mothers or better sex education will do only a little to discourage teenage pregnancy, since many young girls, especially those who have been abused or come from broken homes, are needy and vulnerable and hence easy prey for older men and are often impregnated by rape or incest.

21. Many young women with a chaotic life history get pregnant voluntarily, e.g., to have someone to love them — a behavior not deeply affected by the availability of welfare money or birth control devices.

22. People on welfare would rather make it on their own, since to live off a government check is damaging to their self-esteem and sense of competence.

All 22 of these statements, I suggest, are at least partly true but none may be unequivocally so.[14] Truth and error are nestled together so closely in some of these claims that it is difficult to mark them off from one another. So complex, interwoven, multifaceted, and intricate are the problems associated with poverty and welfare that no conceivable set of policies from the right, left, or center would be a panacea, and all would have ambiguous results. The circumstances of welfare recipients are so varied that hardly any generalization applies to them all, and no remedy would work equally well for everybody. Debaters on every side of the issue come armed with compelling statistics skillfully compiled to justify their own claims. Hardly anything would improve the quality of moral discourse in this country more than a recognition of the complexities and ambiguities of the policy choices we must make.

Let it be said clearly and emphatically, however, that this does not mean that every policy is as good as any other. It is possible to combine a safety net for needy mothers and children while having reasonable and humane work requirements if sufficient employment assistance is provided and decent jobs are made available. But it will be difficult and costly. Or welfare payments could be abolished for able-bodied, competent parents if opportunities for paying work under good conditions were assured in "tough love" ways that did not favor them unjustly in comparison with their similarly situated peers determined to make it on their own. Either option is a major and expensive challenge to policymakers and doubtless exceeds what is politically feasible. Moreover, no matter what we do, frustrating problems will remain, new ones will arise, and some failures will occur. If that is too pessimistic, what is the alternative that (1) is compassionate, (2) will work for everybody, (3) society can afford in light of competing and equally just demands for funds, and (4) is politically doable in today's climate?[15]

ABORTION

Hardly any issue embodies more tormenting ambiguities than the one we consider now. Abortion has polarized society. Extremists on either side argue as if they had the whole truth. For one side, it is simply murder. For the other side, it is plainly a matter of a woman having control over her reproductive capacities or of a woman's right to choose. Pro-life zealots tend to speak only of the fetus — "the unborn child" — and ignore or explain away countervailing circumstances that might surround the situation. A few extremists think it permissible, even obligatory, to kill abortion providers. Pro-choice radicals tend to minimize the moral status of the fetus and are inclined to win too easy a victory over a very difficult problem. A few extremists regard the embryo or fetus as an unwanted parasite or as neutral tissue that can be innocently disposed of, just as one gets a haircut or a fingernail trim. The easy division of people into pro-life and pro-choice camps is itself indicative of the way complex issues full of ambiguities are reduced to simple labels and sound-bite slogans.

The emergence of new life is a continuous process that proceeds over a period of nine months from conception to birth and on into childhood. Designating a point on this unbroken continuum at which a potential person becomes an actual person with all the rights thereunto appertaining is impossible. Everybody agrees that a mother is morally forbidden to kill her child after the fetus has developed into a fully actual person. But at what moment along the way from potential to actual does that prohibition begin to apply? No answer is fully satisfactory. The general rule that the further along in the process abortion occurs, the stronger must be the justification may be correct, but it is vague and offers little precise guidance. Hence, merit attaches to the conservative view that conception itself is the definitive mark beyond which no interference is permissible.

Yet conception itself is a process that takes time to occur, not an instantaneous event. Moreover, not to recognize the difference

111

in fact and moral status between a freshly fertilized egg and a five-year-old child is unconvincing. If a fully actual person is present from conception onward, then the fatal shooting of a doctor who is about to perform an abortion is as morally justified as is the killing of a madman who is about to murder a kindergarten child, if in both cases no other means is available at the moment to prevent the act. Yet few pro-life advocates would go that far. Why not, if they are to be morally consistent? Would not a strict pro-life position forbid abortion even in the case of rape or incest since an innocent "unborn child" would be murdered?

Several conclusions follow. (1) Moral discourse would be served if both sides recognized the complexity of the problem and admitted that ambiguities abound. Above all, greatly to be desired is humility on each side along with an acknowledgement that those who take the opposite position to one's own are not necessarily satanic or lacking in insight or moral integrity.

(2) The only completely satisfactory solution to the abortion problem is to prevent unwanted pregnancies. Once an undesired conception occurs, an emergency ethic is required that defies the rules of normal moral discourse and introduces complexities, difficulties, and compromises one would prefer to avoid but cannot.

(3) Some abortions may be justified, but all abortions inevitably have an element of the tragic and dimensions of moral ambiguity.

(4) Justification for abortion must always be serious and never trivial. Its casual or routine use as a backup or substitute for contraception is morally defective.

(5) The slogan that suggests that abortion should be legal, safe, and rare is probably as good a compromise as the situation allows.

(6) Pro-life advocates ought to be zealous in promoting effective birth control methods to prevent unwanted pregnancy. Pro-choice advocates ought to be aggressive in their efforts to promote sexually responsible behavior, including abstinence, to prevent unwanted pregnancy. Pro-life and pro-choice advocates ought to strive to surpass each other in doing whatever is necessary to reduce the need for abortion to the absolute minimum.

Even if we got agreement that abortion ought to be legal during the early part of pregnancy, the problems would not end there.

Should unmarried teenage girls under, say, seventeen years of age be compelled to secure parental permission before they have an abortion? Should they be free to make this decision on their own? Do parents have a right to know when a young daughter still under their care is about to undergo such a serious procedure? Regardless of which side the law takes on this issue, some good will result, and some harm will be done. Should a compromise be made so that if parents refuse the required permission, a teenage girl may seek an exception from a judge? That might help, but consider that the applicant is then subject to whatever biases a particular judge may have, as well as to the delay and burden of seeking legal aid.

MERCY KILLING

My wife was a chaplain in a Pennsylvania hospital when a young man was brought into the emergency room badly burned in a motorcycle accident. He was in great torment and agony. He had no chance of survival whatsoever. Despite all doctors could do, his condition was horrendous. He remained conscious. He wanted to die. His family stood helplessly by in horror watching him suffer and slowly slip away. Should he be put out of his misery? It would seem to be an act of mercy for somebody who would — and did — inevitably with known certainty die in a matter of hours. Yet deliberately to kill someone is against the law and offends the conscience. We have a term that puts the dilemma before us — mercy killing. The moral law tells us to be merciful, but it forbids us to kill. What shall we do? Good and evil are inseparably intertwined, and the consequences are tragic.

FREEDOM AND THE INTERWEAVING
OF THE ELEMENTS OF EVIL

Four faces of evil have been defined and illustrated — sin, the demonic, the tragic, and the ambiguous. It may be useful to suggest how they are interwoven in the fabric of life and to look at how human freedom is related to these complex relationships. How is freedom related to the origin and overcoming of the various forms of evil?

1. The Tragic: The tragic is unavoidable or irredeemable suffering and evil. If something is totally tragic, then by definition we have no control at all over it, either to prevent it or to redeem it. No matter what choices we make, we cannot reclaim the loss. We are not responsible for the tragic: some disease, unpreventable accidents, tornadoes destructive of life and property, being injured on the highway by a drunk driver, and so on. Most tragedy is not absolute. We have some power to prevent it and some ability to overcome it. While freedom is limited in the extent to which suffering can be redeemed, no prior limits should be put on the capacity of human creativity to endow the apparently pointless with meaning and to bring good out of evil, given sufficient resources of grace and personal strength.

Perplexing questions arise when the sinful and the tragic appear to be mixed, as in the case of the demonic. Moreover, if the Augustinians are correct in teaching that sin is inevitable but that we are nevertheless still held responsible, this is truly tragic. Paul Tillich says explicitly that moral evil is the "tragic implication" of freedom. I argued in a previous chapter for a view of "tragic sin" to designate extreme and probably rare situations in which persons have been so battered by life that they have lost power to do good in some circumstances and instead unavoidably do evil. At least partial redemption may still be possible in some instances. The requirement is a sufficiently powerful experience of being absolutely and unconditionally loved under circumstances that (1) permit or cause the awfulness of their deeds to burst into awareness and that (2) make attractive positive alternatives available to such doomed souls.

2. The Demonic: The demonic originates under circumstances involving some dimension of choice but becomes a persisting power that enslaves. People may not be aware of the influence that is deceiving them or of its satanic character. A tragic dimension is involved in the demonic to the extent that those who are bound by the destructive power of the past have their freedom constrained. Yet since the demonic arises in freedom, it can be overcome through freedom. However, we must first be liberated from the diabolic powers, the sinister ideas, and the satanic practices that have exercised their power over us. How does that happen? It takes place when emancipating grace operates in us. This involves more than a simple decision, since we cannot change until we are liberated or, more precisely, are made free by being liberated.

Sometimes patients in therapy are enabled to reexperience the trauma that gave birth to toxic patterns of thought, feeling, and behavior that have caused them grief. This freshly felt pain from the past, when accompanied by insight into the circumstances and causes of their dysfunctional living, along with the expression of the feelings appropriate to the original situation, may enable them to gain freedom from the debilitating powers. They may get in touch with long repressed feelings like anger present since childhood and experience a catharsis that purifies the soul and brings relief. Fresh patterns of more healthy living become possible when this anger is finally expressed in the context of gaining understanding of its source, meaning, and its destructive effect.

To use another image, light must shine in the darkness. The evil must be seen and known as evil at a deep level. Sometimes this occurs as a result of revelatory experiences. A member of an extremist organization resigned when he realized that if the group came to power, his severely retarded child would be exterminated. This led him to see the disastrous implications of his former belief system.

Conversion is often experienced as a gift from a redeeming influence from beyond our own capacities. Anyone who has ever undergone a liberating experience in therapy or experienced a deep spiritual emancipation can testify to this. As new and more fulfilling ways of thinking, feeling, and acting become attractively available, the oppressive powers can be cast out.

When evil social practices are involved, they must be overcome by good practices. This may require the use of power, and often it involves political means. Sometimes violence must be used, as in the war against Hitler. Slavery in the South was ended by proclamation backed up by military force. Segregation was overcome by a civil rights movement involving masses of people that was effective in securing legislation that brought about needed change. Meanwhile, the slow growth of ideals in the hearts of people prepared the way for eventual peaceful accommodation and final acceptance. Southern politicians now seek votes from African-Americans and proclaim their allegiance to civil rights for all — eloquent testimony to the possibility and fact of moral progress. Granted this new situation may involve elements of political necessity under new circumstances as well as growth in moral sentiment. Hence, social demons may be exorcised gradually by evolution toward higher ideals or by revolutionary upheaval involving the use of force.

3. The Ambiguous: To the extent that good and evil are so bound up with each other that we cannot have the good we want without the evil we don't want, a tragic element is involved. If trade-offs are necessary, we can ask which option on the whole produces the greatest net gain. Freedom, then, can eliminate some of the worst bargains but may not be able to achieve an unequivocal good.

The ambiguous may also involve other dimensions of the tragic. When we claim that what is partly good is totally good because of invincible ignorance involving no fault of our own, the tragic is involved. The sinful gets mixed up with the ambiguous when people take one side on an issue and claim that all the right is on their side. Self-interest may lead us to claim that our truth is the whole truth. The demonic may enter when we are so in the grip of what we have been taught that we honestly think we are right when we are only partially right. We may be morally blind but unaware that we are.

4. Freedom and Unfreedom: A line exists between being unable and being unwilling to choose the good or the best trade-off that is available. That line is sometimes hard to draw. Obviously, some suffering arises from a mixture of human irresponsibility (freedom) and non-human factors (nature). Individuals are in part responsible for their own suffering, as well as for the injustice they do to others. By their foolish, inept, or irresponsible choices, they bring misery upon themselves and their neighbors. Sin occurs when individuals are *unwilling* to choose the better instead of the worse alternative. A tragic dimension enters when they are *unable* because of ignorance or personal deficiency to do the best that could be done in a given situation. Sometimes people hurt themselves and others when they most deeply want to do what is right and good but don't know how or lack the requisite ability to do so. Hence, suffering and injustice may result from sin or exhibit elements of tragedy — or both. Unhappiness experienced in marriage may involve both sin and tragedy.

Life is full of examples of ordinary good people doing the best they can with the best of intentions toward all but who, because of a lack of personal skills, accidents, disease, the perfidy of others — and a host of unavoidable vicissitudes — may end up leading disappointing, miserable lives. Parents do unintentional psychological damage to their children due to distortions in their own behavior rooted in a tortured past that encompasses many generations of interwoven freedom and destiny. Children starve in Africa for a combination of reasons involving both natural forces and historical factors that intermingle the sinful and the tragic in bafflingly complex ways.

In the summer of 1996 violence broke out once more in Northern Ireland. A friend of mine visiting there asked a local citizen what the conflict between Protestants and Catholics was all about. The respondent began by citing an event that occurred in 1082, more than nine hundred years ago![16] Against some social ills with their long sinful, tragic, and demonic history, the forces of reason and good will often seem impotent indeed. The violent acts of extremists on both sides may perpetuate old hatreds and ignite new ones, making it almost impossible for the peace-hungry majority to effect reconciliation. Across the years human life exhibits a complexity and a mystery of iniquity that defies rationality nearly to the point of producing despair in the tender-hearted.[17] Nevertheless, persistence in peacemaking will doubtless in time heal the bloody wounds of Northern Ireland. What Yitzhak Rabin and Yasser Arafat set out to do in seeking peace between Jews and Arabs illustrates the hopeful possibilities that inhere in the most tragic and demonic of situations.

CONCLUSION

Four faces of evil have been described. What is the relationship of God to sin (and injustice), the demonic, the tragic, and the ambiguous? A full answer would require nearly the whole of Christian doctrine, since the good news is God's victory over sin and evil in Jesus Christ and the promise of ultimate redemption from all suffering in the end. The next chapter will set forth a doctrine of God who is perfect in love but limited in power, a God who, as Creator, is indirectly responsible for all evil but directly the cause of no unequivocal evil. The adventure of God in history, however, is caught up in the interweaving of good and evil, as is our own. I will argue that God as Redeemer is opportunistically active in every event, seeking the best possible under the circumstances, but lacks the unilateral capacity to bring about the highest possible good.

---

1. *The Detroit News* (October 14, 1976).

2. The definition of the tragic offered here is my own. For the way in which the category has been employed in philosophy and literature, see Walter Kaufman, *Tragedy and Philosophy* (Princeton: Princeton University Press, 1979). For usage of the tragic closer to mine, see Daniel Day Williams, *The Demonic and the Divine* (Minneapolis: Augsburg Fortress, 1990), 55-71.

3. Given the two factors, four situations of suffering arise. Systematically considered, a dimension of the tragic is present in three:

Avoidable and redeemable	NO TRAGEDY INVOLVED
Avoidable and irredeemable	RELATIVELY TRAGIC
Unavoidable and redeemable	RELATIVELY TRAGIC
Unavoidable and irredeemable	ABSOLUTELY TRAGIC

4. Systematically considered, one feature of tragedy is unavoidable suffering. Three sub-categories arise:

Self-inflicted:	**Situational:**	**Other-inflicted:**
unintentional	arising from	and
or	value conflict	undeserved.
unavoidable.	or from nature.	

118

5. Some will wonder if a God who could not prevent her from being born ugly is of much value and a source of much hope. I see the point. But which is worse, a God who wanted to but could not or a God who could have but did not? Ah yes, but comes the rejoinder: God had a secret purpose in her being born that way that will eventually be seen to have been for the best. I don't accept that view any longer.

6. Reinhold Niebuhr, *The Nature and Destiny of Man*, One vol. ed. (New York: Charles Scribner's Sons, 1949), II:35-97.

7. See *The Washington Post National Weekly Edition* (June 12-18, 1995), 7, and (July 3-9, 1995), 21. For more detailed analyses of income trends and economic opportunities in recent years, see Sheldon H. Danziger, et al., eds., *Confronting Poverty: Prescriptions for Change* (Cambridge: Harvard University Press, 1994). See also, Lester C. Thurow, *The Future of Capitalism: How Today's Economic Forces Shape Tomorrow's World* (New York: William Morrow & Co., 1996).

8. Richard C. Leone, "Taking 'Common' out of Commonwealth," *The Nation* (July 31/August 7, 1995), 130-134. For an analysis of how complexities in the economic order are matched by complexities in the political order, see E. J. Dionne, Jr., *They Only Look Dead: Why Progressives Will Dominate the Next Political Era* (New York: Simon & Schuster, 1996). See also, Michael Lind, *Up From Conservatism: Why the Right Is Wrong for America* (New York: The Free Press, 1996) 138-155, 235-258.

9. For a perceptive analysis of the past few decades, see E. J. Dionne, Jr., *Why Americans Hate Politics* (New York: Simon & Schuster, 1991).

10. I am told that President Harry Truman once said that all he ever heard from his economic advisors about every policy was, "On the one hand, these good results will follow, and, on the other hand, these bad consequences will result." He longed for a "one-handed" economist.

11. *The New York Times* (March 31, 1996), E3.

12. I have explored many of the tensions, complexities, and ambiguities that arise in trying to increase liberty, equality, and the common good simultaneously in *Process Ethics: A Constructive System* (Lewiston: Edwin Mellen Press, 1984), 195-310.

13. I have dealt with the complexities of equal opportunity and affirmative action in considerable detail in *The Passion for Equality* (Totowa, NJ: Rowman &

Littlefield, 1987), 99-128. Three books that respectively argue that with respect to affirmative action we should end it, mend it, or defend it are Terry Eastland, *Ending Affirmative Action: The Case for Colorblind Justice* (New York: Basic Books, 1996); Richard D. Kahlenberg, *The Remedy: Class, Race and Affirmative Action* (New York: New Republic/Basic Books, 1996); and Barbara R. Bergmann, *In Defense of Affirmative Action* (New York: New Republic/Basic Books, 1996).

14. See Lawrence M. Mead, *The New Politics of Poverty: The Non-Working Poor in America* (New York: Basic Books, 1992); Michael B. Katz, *Improving Poor People: The Welfare State, The "Underclass," and Urban Schools as History* (Princeton: Princeton University Press, 1995); Joel F. Chandler, *The Poverty of Welfare Reform* (New Haven: Yale University Press, 1995); Herbert J. Gans, *The War Against the Poor: The Underclass and Antipoverty Policy* (New York: Basic Books, 1995); Charles Murray, *Losing Ground: American Social Policy, 1950-1980* (New York: Basic Books, 1984); Christopher Jencks, *Rethinking Social Policy: Race, Poverty, and the Underclass* (Cambridge: Harvard University Press, 1992); and Mickey Kaus, *The End of Equality* (New York: New Republic/Basic Books, 1992), 103-148. See also, "Symposium: Illegitimacy and Welfare," in *Society* (July-August, 1996), 10-45, containing brief statements by sixteen prominent experts in the field. Finally, see a review of the years 1993-1996, outlining why welfare reform failed this time by David T. Ellwood, "Welfare Reform as I Knew It," *The American Prospect* (May-June, 1996), 22-29.

15. While these words are being written (July 25, 1996), Congress is about to put on the President's desk a bill that he may sign. In my opinion that legislation takes us backward toward worse policies not forward toward better ones, but those who dominate in both parties believe this is what will get them reelected. President Clinton would like nothing better than to rob candidate Dole of the welfare issue.

16. I am grateful to Kenneth Dean for this story he told me on July 15, 1996. I am unable to document whether the reference to the year 1082 points to some significant event in this long story, but it at least illustrates how in the minds of people present ills have their roots in the distant past. This fact itself is important.

17. Some material in the preceding paragraph has been taken from *Theological Biology,* 262-263.

Chapter Seven

God, Evil, And Hope:
Opportunistic Love Overcoming Evil

I knew when I saw him coming that something was wrong. I didn't know the news was that bad. I was about fourteen years old at the time. I had a friend whose name was Alfred Graham. He was two or three years older than I, but we spent a lot of time together. Alfred's father bought a motorcycle. After a time, Alfred learned to ride it and actually gave me a lesson or two. I only rode it once by myself down the road about a half a mile and back. Soon tragedy struck. One Saturday, Alfred's father was doing some work around the house and needed some nails. He got on the motorcycle and rode into town to make the purchase. We all lived out in the country in those days. On the way back, he was in an accident that killed him instantly.

At that time, my mother, my father, and I had taken the job of cleaning the little country church where we were all members. That Saturday afternoon we were getting things ready for Sunday when Alfred came to tell us that his father had been killed. It was a very sad time. I shall never forget being in Alfred's house that weekend and hearing his mother crying out in her agony. Over and over, she screamed, "Why, why, why?" Those words sank deeply into my head and heart. I have often thought about those agonizing words as I pondered the question of suffering, accidents, and tragedy in the light of Christian faith.

In particular, I have wondered just what Alfred's mother meant by her question. What exactly was she asking? What kind of answer was she looking for? What could anyone have said that would have been a satisfactory reply? I don't know, of course, exactly what was in her mind. I have struggled with her question and with the various answers one might give. Nothing would have wiped away her sorrow. In one sense, she was not looking for anyone to take away her pain with some kind of intellectual response. It was, in part, simply a way of expressing her deep distress and anguish in the face of the unanswerable. Yet decades later her question still worries me. What can we say from this distance in the light of all that is involved?

At one level, a clear and simple answer is available. We know *why* it happened if why means how. Mr. Graham was coming down Hill Street at the edge of town. A truck was in front of him. He pulled over into the left lane to pass. As he began to pull around, the truck made a left turn. He ran into the back of the truck. His skull was split, killing him at once. I am sure that her question was not simply about the sequence of events that led up to the accident. Much more remains to be dealt with.

At another level, perhaps she was asking, "Why me? Why him? Why us? Why now, when things are going so well? Why now, when we thought we had many more years together? Why, when he was in the prime of life with so much to live for?" We are in a much more difficult realm now. We are talking about meaning and purpose. We could, of course, say that accidents can happen to anyone. Tragedy is no respecter of persons. No guarantees are available for anybody. No security can be purchased that will preserve us from disaster. Things like that occur. They can happen to anyone at any time. No one of us knows what we may face before the day, or the week, or the year is over. When we read in the papers about some terrible thing, don't we frequently say to ourselves, "There, but for the grace of God, or there, but for good fortune, go I." We know deep down that it could happen to us; yet when it does happen, we cannot help but ask as Alfred's mother did, "Why?" We all knew that if Mr. Graham or the truck had for some reason been 45 seconds earlier or later in arriving at that very spot on Hill Street, it would not have happened. He and the truck were there in that crucial space at the same instant. Still we must press our question on a deeper level. "Why?"

GOD AND OUR SUFFERING

A final level has to do with the ultimate question of meaning and purpose in relationship to our faith in God. In this context, the question is whether God intended anything in what happened. Did God directly and immediately cause it for some reason? Did God arrange just that combination of circumstances, so that Mr. Graham and the truck would arrive at that precise moment? Was God responsible for the fact that the truck turned just as Alfred's father pulled around to pass?

I cannot believe that God directly and immediately causes things like this to happen. I take such a position with all humility. The mysteries of God are beyond our understanding. It would be the height of arrogance to say that I *know* what God does and does not do in particular cases. Beyond that I know that strong theological traditions say otherwise. Many of us have been taught that every event is under God's control. Nothing happens but that God intends it or permits it or causes it.

Contrary to that way of thinking, I have come through many years of struggle and thought to the conclusion that it is wrong to say that God directly and immediately causes every event to happen as it did. God is, of course, indirectly and ultimately responsible for what happens, since God created the world and determined how it would operate. Some distance, however, lies between God and creation. An intervening area must be recognized between God's general control over the world and the specific and particular things that actually happen. This intervening distance means that we have some freedom of action in which we determine what happens. By our own choices a chain of events is set off that sometimes results in good consequences and sometimes in catastrophe. In this arena we are free to learn and to grow. We must face the consequences of our choices. Sometimes we make mistakes and have to pay the cost.

Another area of action not immediately determined by the will of God can be located. In the world of nature is to be found a sort of independence in which things happen in accordance with laws, processes, and arrangements that God has built into the world. A set of events takes place that God does not directly cause. This means that it is wrong to think that God manipulates us like puppets on a string.

Why was Mr. Graham in an accident? He was in an accident because in working out his own purposes, he chose to go into town on an errand. He happened to be at that corner on Hill Street at a particular time. Meanwhile, the driver of the truck, carrying out his own purposes, happened to be there at the same time. As a result of these choices and actions, the collision occurred. The laws of nature held. Metal crashed into the tender tissues of a human body. Brains spilled onto the pavement in a sight that made one sick.

If God did not directly and immediately cause this accident, where was God in all of this? Was God involved at all? I believe God was there in at least two ways. *First of all God was present in sorrow and with a broken heart.* God was there as the Suffering Companion who knows and cares, who feels every hurt and every grief of every creature. Jesus tells us that God has numbered the very hairs of our heads. Not a sparrow falls but that God takes notice.

God was present in a second way. *God was there seeking to use that occasion as an opportunity to bring the greatest good out of that situation.* God is present and at work in every event to increase happiness. God wants to bring about the most harmony, peace, and joy that can be had. Can we say how God does this? It might help to think about it this way. God has built into every living being an urge to fulfillment. I began by quoting the philosopher Whitehead who taught that in all life we find a three-fold drive: an urge to live, to live well, and to live better. God has implanted that motivation in us and in every living creature on the face of the earth. When something goes wrong, God is still there, working through that urge.[1] God is present in that striving to bring the best out of the worst. In and through all events divine purpose redirects and remakes life. God wants whatever good is possible under changed circumstances to happen. God can use our tragedy and suffering as an opportunity to deepen our understanding of life and to strengthen our spiritual foundations.

A few years ago, I chanced to be watching a television program called *That's Incredible*. Usually one does not expect to learn much that is religiously important on a program like that. On this particular show, the story was told of a musician who had lost an arm to cancer. He was cast into great depression and despair. He played the saxophone, I believe. That was the way he made his living. His music was a source of great joy to him. All of that was lost. His life seemed to be in ruins. Then an electronic technician made a device that could be attached to the stump of his arm. By connecting this machine to the nerve endings on one end and to the instrument on the other end, it was possible for him to play again. After a lot of practice, he gained his old skill back. He was brought on the stage so that we could watch him get connected to this device. Then he played — beautifully. He obviously was a very happy man. It was as though he had come back from death to life. Then he spoke. His words were quite remarkable. He said, "I would not have my arm back even if I could. Back then, I did not know what life was all about. Since I lost my arm, I have learned so much. I am such a different person that I had rather be where I am now than where I was when I had my arm."

It would be wrong, I think, to say that God arranged things to make this man get cancer in his arm in order to learn these lessons about life. It would be more accurate to believe that the cancer was the result of something going wrong in his body. Surely, God would have preferred the deepening of his spiritual life to occur in a more normal and healthy way, without the loss of his arm. Surely, God was sorry that the pain and misery happened. Nevertheless, it seems completely in accordance with our faith in a loving, caring God to think that God was at work in the opportunity that his illness provided to bring him to a deeper understanding and appreciation of life and love.

How does God work to bring about the best that is possible? One thing can be said. God creates life with a built-in resurrection potential. If all creatures have an urge to live, to live well, and to live better, something more follows. That urge is so strong that when it is frustrated, it seeks ways to overcome obstacles and make the best of the situation. Life keeps coming back from defeat and rises up to try again. When one path is blocked, another is sought.

I didn't see the cartoon. A friend told me about it. It showed a little stick figure arranged to look like a person. Let us call this little person Human. Human was running around having a good time. Then a fist or something like it came down and crushed this little creature. Soon Human got up and started running again. A bigger fist came down and mashed Human right into the earth. This time it took a little longer. After a while Human struggled to get up and move once more. The fist got bigger and bigger. The blow got heavier and more devastating. Every time Human came back. It took longer and longer. The feet were a little less steady. Nevertheless, life went on.

Finally, one last assault was made. A huge fist that overflowed the screen came down in a mighty force with a tremendous crashing noise. Human was crushed flat to the surface. All was quiet. No movement could be seen. Human, it appeared, was done for. It was all over. This last slam was too much. We watch. Nothing happens. Just when it appears that it is time to put up a little stone marking the place where the end came, a slight stirring can be seen. Then all is quiet again. After some time, another little commotion is evident. Slowly, gradually, painfully, Human struggles, falls, rises again, and at last stands unsteadily but surely. Then Human walks away.

I think this is what the cross and resurrection symbolize for human life on this earth. Life comes with a built-in resurrection potential that never ceases to look for a way to overcome and press on to success. That urge to live, that drive toward fulfillment of the potential for enjoyment, I believe, is present in all living things. It is displayed in the effort seeds make to sprout and grow into a plant with its leaves spread before the nourishing sun. In the face of adverse conditions, a seed takes advantage of every bit of moisture and food value in the soil and of every other circumstance and uses it for its own purpose to grow to healthy maturity. This

126

opportunism that seeks a way around obstacles is characteristic of all life, including human beings. God is the source and basis of this indwelling impetus toward fulfillment (eros) that will not be quenched until every energy has been exhausted.

My belief, then, is that God takes advantage of every opportunity provided in every situation to increase happiness for all in accordance with the health of the individual soul and the requirements of social justice. God is opportunistic within the limits of the possibilities for good compatible with the facts in a given case. God does not supernaturally orchestrate events from beyond to carry out a secret divine scheme. Surprising, unexpected, unlikely things bordering on the incredible can occur. We should be circumspect about putting limits on what is possible. If someone wants to call these astounding events in which good beyond reasonable expectation blesses our lives miracles, I have no objection. I do not believe in supernatural occurrences, but we should be cautious about drawing the boundaries of the natural that demarcate the possible from the impossible.

I have problems with miracles defined as supernatural interference with the law-abiding character of nature and with human freedom on two grounds. (1) They have not happened in my experience, nor have I observed such happenings in the world around me or in the lives of other people. (2) Supernatural miracles pose for me an insuperable theological problem: How do you account for the relative rarity and seeming arbitrariness of such occurrences? Why don't they happen more often? Why does God interfere supernaturally to benefit some and not others? I have heard no satisfactory answers to the questions. The usual and appropriate response is that God has purposes not known to us, and we must simply trust in God's wisdom. The notion that God has secrets that we cannot be let in on is unsatisfactory to me. Equally unsuitable is the idea that God manipulates events from the outside to deliver some but to let others perish. Such beliefs attribute to God mysterious ways of acting that are unworthy of a God of pure boundless love, in my view.

What, then, is our consolation in the midst of tragedy and suffering? We can say at least two things. The first is that God suffers with us as the Loving Companion who is always near, who always cares, who feels our hurts and knows our sorrows. The second thing to be said is that God never ceases to work in all things through the processes of nature and through our freedom to bring the greatest possible good out of every situation.

When tragedy and suffering come, we cannot help asking, "Why?" We can never fully answer that question in a way that quenches our perplexity. Life is full of meaning. Life is also full of mystery. We can be assured with some confidence that God is with us in all things. God gives us the gift of existence and builds into life an urge toward living to the fullest. God is with us to share all our sorrows and our joys. As the Creator, God instills into every life an urge to make use of every opportunity to actualize the potential for good with which we are born. As the Redeemer, God continues to work to bring new good out of evil, new life out of death, hope out of despair, and resurrection from every cross. Such consolation does not remove the heartache and pain. It does provide us with the courage to keep on living and trying, knowing that we are not alone.

IS GOD LIMITED?

Here an objection must be met. I have set forth a view of God perfect in love but limited in power. I have suggested that God works in and through the structures and processes of nature, history, and human freedom. God suffers with us in our tribulation and takes advantage of every opportunity and circumstance to promote our well-being. This means, however, that God's power is limited by the law-abiding character of nature and by the fact of human freedom. If God does not temporarily suspend or overrule the laws of nature and if human beings have the capacity to initiate chains of events and thus produce novelty, then to that extent, God's control is restricted. Many Christians will demur at that point because it denies that God is all-powerful. Christian tradition has taught that God controls all things right down to the specifics of individual events. God causes, permits, or otherwise arranges whatever happens so that in every event God is in full command of everything at all times. This God knows no bounds except those imposed by self-contradiction. God cannot make a short, straight stick with only one end, and the like. However, God can create worlds, control the winds and the seas, and raise the dead. Kicking and screaming and resisting all the way, I have come to reject this view as not fitting as well with the facts of experience as the notion of a finite God who is limited by nature and by human freedom.

Much in the Bible supports the view of God as the Almighty Power, omnipotent and omniscient. Hence, I cannot claim that the Bible as a whole supports me in my view of a limited God. The dominant view is otherwise. Nevertheless, reflection on Scripture and experience has led me against my will to a doctrine of a finite, suffering, struggling God.[2] God, I believe, has a hard time too. There are limits to what God can accomplish on earth. Because God loves, God agonizes with the world and with all human beings in their torment. The only God I can believe in is a God with a broken heart, a God who weeps, who is our companion and support. God is the Fellow-Sufferer who shares our grief, who feels the pain of our sorrows.[3]

To those who object that a finite God does not offer a sufficient basis for hope, I reply that my limited Deity has accomplished as much in this world as the Omnipotent Lord of Christian tradition. No less good and no more evil is to be found in the world in which my Suffering, Struggling, Compassionate Companion lives out the divine adventure than in the world ruled over down to the last tiniest detail by Calvin's Almighty God. We all live in the same world. It is this very world with its promises and perils, its monstrous horrors and its delightful pleasures, that has to be accounted for. I tentatively and in fear and trembling maintain that my theory works as well or better than the alternatives when all that counts and matters is factored into our thinking. To a fuller doctrine of hope, we now turn.

HOPE

If we ask what hope means specifically in our lives today, the answer can be put under three headings. **A.** We can triumph spiritually over suffering in the midst of suffering. **B.** We can change some things for the better here and now. **C.** We can live in the hope that life will be perfected in a realm beyond this world. To put the same points in different words, we can transcend the actual, transform the actual, and live in hope that the actual will be ultimately perfected. Let me spell this out more systematically.

A. Transcendence of the actual.

1. *Fulfillment of the self-transcending moment.* We refer to these occasional moments as "mountaintop experiences" — brief periods when we spontaneously rise above what is actually happening to experience an ecstatic moment of joy in loving union with God, the world, and each other. They don't last long, and they come only now and then. When they appear, it feels like a gift. Shortly, we have to go back down the mountain into real life with all its sin, its tragedy, its demonic dimensions, and its ambiguous decisions. Nevertheless, we can hope that now and then we will transcend it to experience another level of joy and happiness. Sometimes when the tragic and the demonic and the ambiguous cannot be changed, at least in the present moment, we can occasionally rise above these negative dimensions of life.

I remember an occasion four decades ago when the goodness of life broke into my own awareness with particular vividness. It was for me a rare moment of mystical ecstasy. I was walking from a classroom at Emory University to my apartment. It was one of those crisp days in March when the cloudless sky was totally blue. The sun was shining in all its Georgia brightness. The mixture of warmth and coolness told all that Spring was already awakening the dormant earth. I walked through a grove of pine trees and heard the wind softly breathing through the thick branches. All of a sudden and unexpectedly, I felt a surge of good feeling. It can only be described as an acute, deep awareness of the pure joy of being alive. It was as if the pine trees and all of nature shared the experience. All around me was the busy world of living and dying. Not far away was a little shopping center where people bought food, clothes, and medicine. About a block in the distance was Emory Hospital where people of all ages and of all races and of all stations in life were suffering and dying. The world in all of its beauty and pain was still there. Nevertheless, in my little cathedral in the pines I knew for a brief few moments what it meant for Genesis to proclaim that God looked at the world still fresh and pure and saw that it was good, very good.

2. *The experience of blessedness in the midst of suffering.* This is not transient and occasional like the first but a more or less continuous triumph over suffering, while the suffering continues (Romans 8:31-39). Nothing can separate us from the love of God. Peril, famine, sword, fire and flood, the unjust, the demonic, the ambiguous, and the tragic are all around, but the awareness that God suffers with us is a comfort in our tribulation. Not all of us can achieve this blessedness all the time, but it is a possibility for which we hope in the midst of pain, injustice, and tragic affliction.

B. Transformation of the actual.

Some things in actual life can be changed to make them better. We cannot bring about perfection in this life, but we may be able to improve them. Some problems can be solved, or at least partially so. If we are sick, we can hope to get better. If there is injustice, we may be able to change things to make them more just. If there is hatred, we can work for reconciliation. Demonic powers can, under the right circumstances, be cast out and overcome, at least in part. Trade-offs will often be unavoidable, so that we get something good only by having to take something bad along with it. Compromises are inevitable, but we can work for a better bargain that gets more of the good and less of the evil. Sometimes we have to take the lesser of two evils, but we can try to lessen the evil of the lesser evil. Some suffering can be relieved, and it is our obligation to overcome as much of it as we can. The unjust, the tragic, the demonic, and the ambiguous can in some circumstances be at least partially overcome, thus transforming the actual situation for the better.

Especially important in this connection are those *kairotic*[4] moments in history and in our personal lives in which the times are ripe and ready for constructive change. A convergence of factors may produce a situation that is pregnant with new possibilities, requiring midwives to facilitate the birth. Such an opportunity presented itself in the eighteenth century when the American

Revolution produced "a new nation conceived in liberty and dedicated to the proposition that all men (people) are created equal" (Abraham Lincoln). Philosophers had produced doctrines of human rights and of democratic rule. The social and economic circumstances of European settlers living in a new land imbued with such notions enabled them to take advantage of the opportunities to create a fledgling democracy with great promise. It was an imperfect union that centered on the prerogatives of white, property-owning males. It assumed African slavery and the inferiority of Native Americans. Its flaws have not yet been overcome. The new nation flourished at the expense of killing and pushing Native Americans from the land, destroying their culture in the process. Nevertheless, although accompanied by deep ambiguities and profound evils, the total situation exhibited dimensions of progress in the course of civilization.

Another situation pregnant with promise for the increase of justice and happiness occurred during the 1950s during the Civil Rights Movement. A complex constellation of factors coalesced to create possibilities for advancing the cause of justice that simply had not been present a quarter of a century before. Dr. Martin Luther King, Jr., along with many others, were ready and able to convert these opportunities into genuine gains that transformed the South in particular but the rest of the country as well. Racism in forms brutal and subtle remains, but genuine progress has occurred.

Our task is to be alert to those places in individual and social life where these right and ripe moments arise and then to take advantage of them to turn possibility into fact. Every new advance is associated with possible new evils and persisting old ones, but in the process lines of material, social, and moral amelioration can be traced. These advances are worth striving for and can make an enormous difference in the lives of people. Progress is potential in the historical process though not guaranteed. To actualize this potential in real gains of justice and joy is a moral imperative.

C. The perfection of the actual.

This is the final and ultimate dimension of hope. The first two are either temporary or partial. The sinful, the tragic, the ambiguous, and the demonic are still real, but we can occasionally or to some extent overcome them, but they are still present in fact. The Bible and Christian faith say something more. God works for a final victory when all suffering will be ended. All evil will be put down. Good will triumph once and for all and completely. The imperfect will be made perfect. Then there will be no more tears, no more pain, no more death. (Revelation 21:1-4; 1 Corinthians 15). Oppression of the weak and the outcast, tragedy, enslavement to evil powers, and thorns on the roses will be gone, eliminated.

How such a complete victory of good over evil could come to pass is unknown to us. The forms of a totally transformed life are hidden from our view. That it is even possible is not certain.[5] That it will in fact happen is not an assured fact. A more modest hope would be to forego the notion of a final perfection and to rest content in the faith that God works ceaselessly and opportunistically to lure the world forward into creative advance. Perhaps sin, the tragic, the ambiguous, and the demonic cannot be totally rooted out of any finite world. Yet the hope of heaven is so attractive that it is difficult to eradicate from the human heart. Trust in divine love at the end is the final recourse of the human spirit.

Part of Christian discipleship is discernment. We must read and understand the signs of the times. We need to be sensitive to the situations we face and rejoice in the hope that is appropriate to each situation, taking into account all the circumstances that prevail at the moment. Sometimes a bad situation can be changed for the better. Sometimes it cannot. When it can, hope urges us to work militantly for the best transformation that is possible in the lives of individuals and in society. When the actual situation cannot be changed for the moment, we can hope for a triumph over the actual situation, to experience a spiritual victory in the midst of wrongdoing, famine, peril, and sword. Finally, beyond this life Christian hope looks for the perfection of the world — an ultimate once and for all victory over all suffering.

A final chapter taken from my own experience will show how the categories that have been employed throughout this essay have illuminated the meaning of my own life.

---

1. My inspiration comes primarily from Alfred North Whitehead, but compare what I have said with Paul Tillich. "Providence is a *quality* of every constellation of conditions which 'drives' or 'lures' toward fulfillment ... the quality of inner-directedness in every situation." *Systematic Theology* (Chicago: University of Chicago Press, 1951), I:267.

2. The theological method I employ and my view of biblical authority can be found in my *Toward a New Modernism* (Lanham, MD: University Press of America, 1996), vii-xi, 1-76. For me the norm of theological thinking is the best we know from all sources up to now, the Bible and Christian tradition being chief among them. Put otherwise, all theological claims must be measured in the last analysis by canons arising from our own fallible, culturally conditioned reason and our own limited experience. For those who demand a stricter adherence to biblical themes or to traditional theology, my approach will not be acceptable. Yet I argue that the interpretive element is strong in all outlooks and that there is no such thing as a pure reading off of objective truth from unerring sources, uncontaminated by subjective judgment. We all walk by faith and not by sight. In the end I am a relativist and a pragmatist who has given up the hopeless quest for an unimpeachable certainty and settled for tentative, working hypotheses that provide understanding and means of coping with life within my own frame of reference. See the book itself for an acknowledgement of the weaknesses in my position, a critique of alternatives, and the grounds for my own approach.

3. I have developed this view technically and in more detail in *Toward a New Modernism*, 77-107, and in *Theological Biology: The Case for a New Modernism* (Lewiston: Edwin Mellen Press, 1991), 233-289. See also, *Science, Secularization and God* (Nashville: Abingdon Press, 1969). A collection of sermons assuming a finite, suffering God can be found in *The Triumph of Suffering Love* (Valley Forge: Judson Press, 1966).

4. The Greek word *kairos* means special occasion, proper or convenient time, season of opportunity. Theologians use it to refer to a right and ripe moment when something new, good, and momentous can break forth into reality. A *kairotic* occasion contains a significant potential for a novel birth of meaning, goodness, or justice.

5. For many years I have posed this question: If heaven is possible, why not now? No answer I have ever heard is convincing. Earlier, I speculated that any world composed of a plurality of interacting finite, free beings in a law-abiding world will contain the possibility of evil that is likely to occur. Can there be free, finite beings in a world with perfect good and no evil? If so, why not now? Yet it would be foolish to deny that there may be possibilities of perfection unknown and unknowable to us that may yet come to pass. We walk by faith in hope as we seek to increase love for God and of neighbor.

Chapter Eight

It's Okay, Life Must Go On!

Here is a letter a father wrote to his children on the first anniversary of their mother's death.

October 19, 1988

Dear Paul, Nancy, and Melissa,

It was a year ago this week that your mom died. I am not sure what to say, but I felt we needed to take some notice of this together. I hope this letter may be a means of our sharing some thoughts and feelings even though we are far away from each other.

This has been a hard year for us. Every holiday, anniversary, and birthday has been a reminder of our loss. I miss her very much. I don't cry as much as I did. Now it is mainly when something triggers a memory — driving by the Plymouth Avenue exit that leads toward Mt. Carmel House, seeing the beautiful leaves and knowing how much she would have enjoyed them, things like that. It has taken most of this year to recover a sense of equilibrium and somehow to be able to go on and enjoy life. Last year after returning from the funeral, I was walking around outside Saunders House in the parking lot. I suddenly had a sense of your mom's presence. She was saying to me, "I'm all right. It's okay for you to be happy, to carry on your life." That was very reassuring. But as I look back I realize that it was not until late this summer that I was really prepared to go ahead and try to live life to the fullest. Gloria and I went to church in Griffin on August 14. Bruce Morgan's topic was "The Show Must Go On." He told the biblical story of King David, whose son, Absalom, was killed in battle. He grieved and grieved until at last someone in effect told him, "Life must go on. You have a kingdom to rule." That message came to me at the right time. Only then was I able to hear it and to know that it was okay for me to be happy, to get on with life.

All last winter I felt disjointed and out of sorts with the world, irritable, cynical. Nothing felt right. I was alienated from my job, religion, everything else just about. I am sure my illness of three months was somehow tied into all this. It has only been since going to Georgia and returning that I have felt whole again, really excited about my writing, happy in my job, etc. Grief takes a long time. Healing is slow, but it is coming.

It would be dishonest to cover up all the differences your mom and I had. I left, and we were divorced. That is the fact. We had a lot of anger and alienation. I am very glad to say that during the last months of her life, we really did experience a deep and complete reconciliation, and we said as much to each other as I sat holding her hands through the bars of her bed at Mt. Carmel. We agreed that there was nothing more that needed to be said on that score. I was reminded of an old gospel hymn — "That Old Account Was Settled Long Ago."

That made it possible for us to remember the good things. And there were many good things. Your Mom was one of the finest human beings I have ever known. Her integrity and honesty were beyond reproach. There was not a devious or deceitful bone in her body. She was utterly genuine and sincere all the way through. Her love of life was very deep. It was the simple things of family and friends, love of home — she wanted a beautiful home, she once told me more than most anything else — her love of nature, of beautiful scenery, and on and on. Nobody ever loved husband or children more than she. They were first in her life. She had her faults, we all do, but in the very best way she knew how, she devoted her life to us — her husband and her children. She spent hours and hours shopping for all of us, going all over town in snow and rain to find just what she wanted, something she thought we would like. She was never to have the house she wanted or keep it the way she wanted. She just couldn't do what she wanted most. But she tried and I think did the best she knew or could under the circumstances.

We all had painful experiences and have painful memories. But somehow that does not seem as important now as the memory of a kind, gentle, loving person who just wanted to be happy and to make her family happy.

Something she and I shared was our common love for the three of you. We were never divided on that. She was so proud of you, each one of you. She took such great satisfaction in your accomplishments. She loved you very, very much. We sometimes failed you, each of us in our own individual ways, and together as parents we did not provide for you the kind of stable, loving, contented household we both wanted for all of us. All of this has left me with a pretty deep sense of the tragic in life. Here were good people who really loved each other but who did not know how to get what we wanted most. No bad will was present in anybody. We didn't know how or couldn't manage it.

I guess that is the saddest part of it all. Many times I have said and thought, "I wish it could have been better for her." I wish it could have been better for the two of us and for the five of us, but most of all I wish it could have been better for her. The last years with my leaving, your growing up and moving away, her living alone and unable to cope, and finally the illness that conquered her were marked with a lot of loneliness, suffering, depression, and pain. I wish it could have been otherwise. There is a tragic dimension to life, to her life, and to the lives of so many people who only want to be happy and to live their lives out with some satisfaction.

One of the most gratifying and joyful aspects of all this is the way the three of you rallied around your mom during those last months. You were all wonderful in the way you moved in to help and make her last days as comfortable and satisfying as they could be. Equally important is the way you have supported each other. I am so glad for that. I am glad we have all had each other during this difficult year and the one before that when the inevitable was pressing in on us.

I have written this with many tears. I have not written you to make you sad, but I hope that by experiencing and sharing our grief with each other we can move through this. Your mom is saying to all of us, "It's okay. It's okay for you to be happy." Yes, it is okay. Life must go on. I think I am ready for that now. I hope you are too.

We do not know what the future holds. But we do have each other. I love you, each one of you in your own special uniqueness and all of you together, very much. Like your mom, I am very proud of you. We have shared a lot together, and it has drawn us all closer.

I look forward to seeing all of you at Thanksgiving. It will be good to be together. Please accept this letter as a way I could share some deep feelings with you. It has been good for me to write it and to experience what this week means in my memory with you.

I love you very much.
Dad

I am that father, the author of the letter. I took it right off my computer files. The experiences I had during the last 25 years of Eloise's life had as much as anything to do with my understanding of the many faces of evil. Throughout this little volume I have made reference to events and feelings in my inner life and history that theologians writing books on evil do not usually share publically. Most of my own writing on God and evil has sharply separated my personal life from my conceptual conclusions. That is the style of most theological writing. I do not disparage that practice or deny its legitimacy. Yet all of us have a self known to others in public encounter and a self known only to ourselves in introspective reflection. Only in the union of the two can we fully express the whole meaning of life. The knowledge of good and evil resides in its completeness in the depths of the heart. There alone are to be found the inner agonies and ecstasies known only to ourselves as well as the outer travails and triumphs known also to others. The private and the public go together to form the entire fabric of life.

On the public side, I write these words the day after the bombing of the federal building in Oklahoma City in April, 1995. A little more than a year later I make this final review during the month when TWA flight 800 took a fiery plunge into the Atlantic Ocean and when a crude pipe bomb in Centennial Park in Atlanta (July, 1996) shattered the mood of celebration at the Olympic Games and cast a shadow of apprehension over a nation coming to grips with the ever-present possibility of terrorism. In these public events too are the manifestations of the sinful, the demonic, the tragic, and the ambiguous.

It was in the intimate laboratory of life that I came to understand in my heart more than I had ever learned from books or in mere thought about the many dimensions in which this life is troubled. It was all there in my marriage. The sinful was present. While I never had any intent to hurt, not all my actions were wise or kind or helpful. Some of my damaging behavior expressed my own pain, frustration, confusion, and anger. Sometimes it was incompetence in knowing how to respond and relate rather than any moral failing as such, although that was involved too. Separation and divorce created injustice for our children. I divided my income equally with Eloise, but running two households was expensive. Our children were in college and suffered financially. In addition, the resulting pain and suffering they underwent from the breakup of the family was unjust. They did not deserve that loss of the most intimate and nourishing community humans have devised to promote the well-being of children.

Could I have done differently? That question is difficult and one I have often pondered. In some cases, the answer is that I could have. In other instances, I think I was very near the borderline between unable and unwilling without really understanding which most accurately described my actions. At other times, I did what I did because I was who I was. I could not have done differently or better than I actually did in those circumstances at that point in my life. This means that sometimes I did what was actually objectively best under the circumstances, as I honestly understood things. At other times I did the best that I could do, even though it might not have been the best objectively possible as measured by the facts and options available. Frequently, I wanted to do what was objectively best but was not sure what that was, given the situation as it had developed. Human life is complicated, and we must not reduce it to a few unambiguous principles that always apply.

Certainly the ambiguous was present. To ask what is best is not a simple question. Best for whom? Myself? The children? Eloise? Best in what respects? Many choices result in some good consequences and some bad outcomes, with no way to have one without the other. That is a point I have tried to make over and over. I could spell that out with many details from my marriage. One choice, however, stands out and may represent the rest.

After many years of talking, praying, and on occasion seeking professional help, I made a decision to move out in 1979. She would have continued to struggle on, since she believed that a bad marriage was better than a divorce. Had I decided to stay on and struggle with improving the marriage, good and bad would have been mixed up in the consequences. Certainly we would have been better off financially. We had two children in college whom we could have helped more. Melissa could have continued to live with both parents, whereas after I left she moved back and forth between us. In many ways the separation was hardest on her, since she was still living at home. I remember very well what she said when I told her and Nancy in a laundromat in Claremont, California, that I had decided to move out. Immediately she posed a question, "What will happen to me?" What happened to Melissa was a source of great pain to her and to me. Yet Eloise and I had struggled for more than fifteen years with a failing marriage. To continue on would have perpetuated the misery and conflict we had both experienced. For years I had been agonizing over what to do. Finally, on August 1, 1979, I moved into an apartment a few blocks away.

The painful truth is that separation and divorce were liberating for me but devastating and destructive for her. I had hoped that divorce, as torturous as the process would be for us and our children, would eventually prove to be beneficial, all things considered, for both. A therapist had encouraged us to expect that outcome. He said to Eloise, "I'd be willing to bet that if Ken moves out, within a year you'll have a job, and you'll be better off all around." It did not work out that way.

I will not go into all the details, but within a month after I moved out, she was diagnosed with colon cancer. She had surgery and lived cancer free for six years. Another tumor appeared in 1985, requiring more surgery. By the next June diagnosis revealed that the cancer had spread to her liver. After that it was a matter of time. She died on October 21, 1987.

Could she have done differently? Could she have worked out a better life for herself? How responsible was she for her misery? I will not make judgments about that, for I really don't know. It appeared to me that, by and large, she did the best she could under the circumstances with the personal resources and strength of personality she possessed. Maybe she would answer as I did, saying that sometimes she could have done better or differently, and sometimes she could not. Perhaps if she had remained healthy, she might have been able to find a more satisfying life for herself. Divorce and cancer were too much.

That recognition leads us to the tragic dimension. Given her personality and mine and our life histories, I think some of our difficulties and suffering were inevitable, unavoidable, and irredeemable. I have no patience with shallow optimists who glibly proclaim in books, sermons, conferences, and television uplift sessions that all good things are possible for everybody, that life can be beautiful all the time, that happiness and bliss are ours to claim. Usually, there is a catch. All this can be ours — **if only** we will follow some prescription they possess and are eager to supply. To be forthright, most inspirational speakers depress me with their superficial platitudes, their easy, failsafe remedies, and their infallible road maps to utopia.

Life is full of hope and possibilities for redemption. We do not always do the best we can to actualize the real potential for good in situations. Sometimes we could do better than we do. Some of our suffering is self-inflicted and avoidable. Much suffering is redeemable. Of course, all that is true — and more. Nevertheless, there is a point beyond which human frailty cannot take us, a line at which unwilling does pass over into unable. Beyond that point and that line a tragic dimension enters into life. We are limited by the resources of personality we were born with and acquired through nurture, experience, learning, and choice. Sometimes that is not enough to enable us to avoid or redeem all suffering. When we have done the best we could with what we had in the light of our best knowledge and still affliction remains, the tragic enters.

Finally, the demonic was present. Whatever insufficiencies we had from our genetic inheritance that limited our ability to cope constituted part of the tragic dimension. Whatever structural impairment incorporated into our character structure that had its ultimate origin in irresponsible choices, either ours or that of others, constituted a demonic element. Doubtless both factors were present to some degree. I grew up in an unhappy home during my early years. I am sure that the arguments, the screaming and yelling, the accusations, and all the rest I heard at night that resulted in my crying myself to sleep certainly left their mark on me. Perhaps my parents had tragic and demonic components in their own makeup. The demonic passes on from parent to child to grandchild, and so on. Each new generation adds its own failures to the mix.

I am not a psychiatrist, but I have come to understand some of the ways in which what I experienced in childhood handicapped me as a marriage partner. Other demonic influences may have damaged me in ways that I have not yet fully understood. I am happy to say that some of those demons have been exorcised through professional and self-administered therapies, though I am not yet fully whole. To mention one point, long buried anger toward my parents was at last touched, expressed, and robbed of its venom.

The last word must be one of hope. Irresponsibility, ignorance, injustice, the tragic, the demonic, and the ambiguous all contributed to the suffering Eloise, Paul, Nancy, Melissa, and I underwent. Nevertheless, out of it came much that was good. The letter that began the chapter tells part of that story. Eloise and I were brought to complete reconciliation. She died in a hospice, where I visited her every day I was in town until she died. We had long talks amid many tears. Forgiveness and healing of personal wounds are real possibilities. I have experienced it firsthand. My children were drawn closer together, and those bonds remain strong. The way they love each other and come to each other's aid is a joy in my life. My children and I came to love each other even more deeply as we gathered around their mother during those months of her dying. I have reason to believe they have forgiven Eloise and me for the hurt we caused them by our difficulties.

I cared for Eloise during the last year of her life. I paid her bills, bought her groceries and medicine, took her shopping, saw that she got to the doctor. I made arrangements to get her into Mt.

Carmel, where she spent the last five months until her death. I planned her funeral. I took the dress she was buried in to the cleaners and then to the funeral home. I had the slab put on her grave. My children were scattered around the country. All of Eloise's relatives lived in Georgia. I was in every way her primary caretaker. We found a peace and joy with each other in those last months that we had not had since the early years of our marriage.

Let me repeat that I do not believe God arranged for Eloise to be sick and to die so that these good things could come to pass. For God to bring suffering on one person as an instrument to produce good for others is incompatible with divine love. Moreover, the idea that God is working things out in accordance with some foreordained plan unknown to us that we must simply accept on faith is not a part of my theological outlook. I do not believe God manipulates persons and events in this fashion. I do believe that God is at work in all circumstances of life to achieve the highest possible good, but God works in and through the structures and processes of nature, history, and human freedom to accomplish this steady love-motivated aim. God does not violate these regular patterns or interfere from without with the laws of nature or the decisions of human beings. Rather God works through the drive toward fulfillment, the *eros* that urges all life toward the actualization of its built-in potential for enjoyment.

Let me complete my story on a happy and sad note. I have been happily remarried since October, 1984, and I am very greatful for the life Gloria and I have together. And what about my parents who kept me awake at night with their quarreling when I was eight years old? They entered a nursing home in December of 1994 and shared a room. On March 10, 1995, they celebrated 66 years of marriage. It would be difficult to find a more devoted and loving couple. My mother was in the hospital for a few days in October, 1994. I took my father in to visit her. I rolled his wheelchair as close as I could to her bed. Neither spoke, but each extended a hand toward the other. Tears rolled down my cheek as I watched their bony fingers grasp each other and hold on tenderly as they looked into each other's eyes. Redemption is possible, and I was witnessing it. My father was approaching 88 when he died in his sleep on May 1, 1995, after a bout with pneumonia.

I still talk to Eloise now and then. She continues to tell me that she's okay, that everything is all right, and that I should live as fully and as happily as I can. And now when I talk to my dad, he tells me the same thing! Despite everything, life must go on. So it does.

Index